Managing Conflict
in the
Workplace

Sandra D. Collins, PhD

With James S. O'Rourke, IV, PhD, Editor

A ReVision Book

Published by ReVision, LLC
27695 US Highway 20
South Bend, Indiana 46628

ISBN:1945103000
ISBN-13:9781945103001

DEDICATION

To Ron Thomas who offered much needed support during many hours of writing and revising for this and other projects, and to Jim O'Rourke for his invaluable guidance.

CONTENTS

ACKNOWLEDGMENTS

This text brings together for the reader pieces of the work done in the area of conflict management and resolution by many of the greatest contributors to the field, and it is to those researchers, writers, and educators who the greatest acknowledgment. In addition, the stories and examples shared in the book could not have been written without the contributions of colleagues, students, workshop participants, and friends and family, who were willing to share their experiences and challenges in dealing with conflict. Many thanks to you all! You know who you are, but don't worry, because no one else does.

This text was initially part of a seven-book series edited by Professor James S O'Rourke IV, Director of the Fanning Center for Business Communication, Mendoza College of Business, University of Notre Dame.

CHAPTER

1

THE NATURE OF CONFLICT

If you want to avoid conflict at work, you can. All you have to do is find a job that doesn't require you to have any contact with people. If you think that might be difficult for you, then I have some bad news. You're going to experience conflict. Most of us are surrounded by conflict in some form or another every day. Some of this conflict involves us directly, while some we may simply observe. But all of it affects us in some way, just as it affects the organizations we belong to. Though the type of conflict we experience may vary from day to day, one thing remains unchanged: Conflict at work is inevitable. The best you can do is learn to manage it well and, perhaps, even come to appreciate its possible benefits.

Robert Ramsey, a contributing editor at *Supervision* magazine, reports that a survey of 150 executives found that they spend an average of about 18 percent of their work time "acting as a peacekeeper, referee, and mediator" for employees engaged in conflict.[1] Other studies estimate that figure to be as high as 30 percent.[2] That means managers are spending between nine and fifteen weeks a year dealing with conflict in the workplace. A recent study by Integra Realty Resources reported that 42 percent of the workers surveyed have witnessed yelling or other verbal abuse at work, and 29 percent of those surveyed admit to having yelled at co-workers themselves.[3] "Sometimes you just snap," explained one Internet company employee who quit his job a week after losing his temper with his boss and letting loose a stream of obscenities.[4]

What are the causes of workplace conflict? An uncertain economy, threats of downsizing, competition for promotion, misplaced loyalties, finger-pointing over mistakes, and job-related stress are all contributors to workplace conflict. The changing landscape in the modern workplace has brought with it new challenges for keeping peace.[5]

- **Rapid pace of business.** Employees are pushed to produce more in less time, creating more stress and short tempers.
- **Increased competition.** Many factors such as technological advances and an increasingly global economy have intensified the competition in numerous markets.
- **Diversity in the workplace.** Organizations strive toward and benefit from greater diversity. With a more diverse workforce, however, comes the difficulty of people with different perspectives to get along.
- **Flattened organizational structures.** Managers and employees are on more familiar terms than they once were, leading to less formal communication. While this has its advantages, it also increases the likelihood that small courtesies and signs of respect may seem unnecessary.[6]

But perhaps the most universal reason for workplace conflict is simply that people are different. When people work together, it is inevitable that they will sometimes disagree over things like goals, the way to achieve goals, or whether or not one party is capable of achieving a goal and the like.

In this book, we'll talk about two major categories of conflicts: yours and your employees'. No doubt, we all know the consequences doing a poor job of dealing with our own conflicts. And one goal of this book is to help you manage your conflicts more effectively. A second goal is to help you *help your employees* deal with their conflicts more effectively as well.

Conflict Quote

All these different rages—road rage, air rage, whatever rage—are all symptoms of the same thing: We all have too many commitments and too little time.
—Lynne McClure, McClure Associates[7]

When employees clash, it's tempting to wait it out and hope the problem will go away. After all, most managers don't like to interfere in their employees' lives and many feel ill equipped to cope with employee conflict. Some managers fear training their employees to bring their troubles to them automatically, instead of trying to work things out on their own first. Furthermore, sometimes a conflict actually will go away on its own, adding to the appeal of the "do nothing" approach. But sometimes it doesn't. In fact, like a bad cold, conflict can infect an organization as those involved tell others about it.[8] In one study of how employees respond to conflict at work, more than 86 percent of those surveyed said that they discuss it with a co-worker.[9] Conversations of this sort can quickly spread conflict through an organization, disrupt harmony and morale in the workplace, and impede work performance.[10]

Daniel Dana, a mediation specialist and author of *Conflict Resolution*, estimates that 65 percent of performance problems result from conflicts between employees, representing a huge expense for organizations. "Unmanaged employee conflict is perhaps the largest reducible cost in organizations today—and probably the least recognized." Dana includes eight separate factors when estimating the cost of conflicts to an organization, including critical events, such as the loss of skilled employees; restructuring; losses caused by employees through sabotage, theft, or damage; and more commonplace problems such as wasted time, bad decisions, lowered job motivation, absenteeism, and health-related costs.[11]

BEHAVIORAL RESPONSES TO CONFLICT IN ORGANIZATIONS

Conflicts in organizations can lead to a variety of behavioral responses, many of which are counterproductive for the workplace. The most frequent response to conflict at work is verbalization.[12] People involved in workplace conflict like to talk about it. While they sometimes choose to speak directly to the other party in the dispute about the issue, they very often choose to speak to co-workers outside the conflict, and even to people outside the organization.[13]

Behavioral responses to conflict can be classified as direct, indirect, or uncontrollable (see Table 1-1). Discussing the issue with the other party in the conflict would be a direct response, secretly sabotaging the other party's work would be indirect, and crying would be uncontrollable (unless tears were produced strategically). Behaviors can also be classified by intensity of response. Avoiding the other party would be at the low end of intensity and striking the person would be at the high end.[14]

In workplace conflicts that continue over a period of time, people engage in numerous behavioral responses as patterns of behavior emerge. Conflicting parties may try one strategy for dealing with the conflict but switch to another if their initial response is ineffective. A common pattern of responding includes switching from some sort of verbalization (e.g., discussing the issue, shouting at the other party) to helplessness (e.g., crying, not talking to the other party, or ignoring the conflict), and back to verbalization.[15] An example of this pattern might be an employee who initially responds to conflict by complaining to co-workers (verbalization) and avoiding the other party in the conflict (helplessness) but eventually raises the issue with the other party directly (verbalization).

Table 1-1: Popular Behavioral Responses to Conflicts in the Workplace

Direct	Indirect	Uncontrolled
· Discuss with person. · Listen to person. · Try to convince the person. · Shout at the person. · Strike the person.	· Avoid the person. · Discuss with co-workers. · Discuss with people outside the organization. · Talk or joke behind the person's back. · Go to the person's supervisor.	· Show tension nonverbally (clenched jaw, tightened muscles). · Cry.

While forms of verbalization and common patterns of responding can allow employees to develop as people and grow their relationships, an increasingly common form of verbalization, due in part to flattened organizational structures and less formal communication at work, includes acts of incivility or rudeness toward others in the workplace.

5

Common examples of rudeness in the workplace include condescending and demeaning comments, overruling decisions without offering a reason, talking about people behind their backs, not giving credit when credit is due, and giving dirty looks. But rude behaviors can become more serious and can include insulting others, yelling, sexually harassing employees, and even becoming violent.[16]

Simple rude behavior is so commonplace it may seem that managers have little choice but to accept it as part of the changing landscape of work. But rudeness and incivility can spiral into a serious conflict, particularly since people have different definitions of what constitutes rude behavior. A thoughtless act that the instigator did not intend to be perceived as rude may be misconstrued and provoke retaliation. Once the original act is reciprocated with an incivility, the spiral begins. A series of reciprocities can lead to escalation. Small acts and little comments can lead to big problems, even acts of violence.[17] Nationally, there are 18,000 cases of nonfatal violence in the workplace per week, and in 2000, some 599 people in private industry were killed as a result of workplace violence.[18]

Coping with rude behaviors at work can have an impact on worker performance. In one study, 53 percent of targets of rude behavior responded by losing time at work worrying, 28 percent lost time at work avoiding the rude person, and 22 percent decreased their effort at work. Organizations can pay the price for their employees' rudeness in other ways, as well. The poor work environment may lead to chronic physical illness in some employees, high levels of turnover, diminished loyalty, and, in some cases, litigation.[19] Workplace violence is now estimated to cost employers from $6.4 billion to $36 billion annually in lost productivity, reputation damage, insurance costs, and increased security.[20]

trials brought to court

Conflict Quote

> *Aggression in the workplace has a consequence. When you have aggressors in the workplace, other workers don't want to be there. It starts with employee tardiness, then absenteeism, then turnover.*
> —John Byrnes, President, Center for Aggression Management[21]

Employees who feel they are not being treated fairly in an organization may resort to a variety of tactics to relieve their frustration, including at times denigrating their manager. They may tell unflattering stories and jokes about the manager or the organization behind the manager's back. Dissatisfied employees may engage in more overt behaviors as well, including pressure tactics. Employees working together, in both unionized and non-unionized organizations, can apply pressure to management by orchestrating slowdowns, absences, and lower product quality.[22]

The point of all this is simply this: Conflict in the workplace that is not managed well is detrimental and costly to an organization. And as we have already noted, conflict is inevitable. If you are riding this train toward the logical conclusion, you're already thinking that it's a good idea to learn how to manage conflict well if you intend to hold a position of leadership within an organization. The question for managers isn't should I learn how to manage conflict well or even will I need to do that – you should, and you will. Of course, you'll have many opportunities with your own conflicts, but what about those of your employees? The real question for managers is how will I know when will I need to step in?

Because conflict in the workplace is inevitable and, in some ways, even desirable, a manager may have difficulty determining when the nature or intensity of conflict means that intervention is required. Obviously, shouting, threats, or any form of violence will require immediate attention, as does the destruction of property. But behaviors don't have to be this intense to be disruptive to the work environment. When a conflict between two or more employees becomes the "buzz" around the rest of the office, it is probably time to do something. Conflicts that are allowed to continue and aren't managed well can create a tense and uncomfortable environment for employees. Rude behaviors that are disrespectful shouldn't be tolerated. Nor should behaviors that result in slowed performance, like refusing to cooperate or purposely sabotaging efforts.[23]

When conflict begins to affect worker productivity and effectiveness, it needs to be addressed, not ignored. While not all conflicts will get to the point of requiring a manager's intervention, some will, and a good leader can plan for that and be ready when it occurs. Managing workplace conflict is much like any other managerial skill: It can be learned and developed. An unprepared manager who uses a "wait and see if it gets out of control" strategy for dealing with employee conflict will be ineffective at best.[24] Good preparation involves developing an understanding of conflict, learning ways of analyzing conflicts, and practicing techniques for the resolution and management of conflict, both for yourself and your employees.

THE NATURE OF CONFLICT

We have already made the point that conflict is inevitable. Here's another fact about conflict: Most people find it unpleasant. At the root of this unpleasantness is fear. Fear of upsetting someone, fear of being upset, fear of losing control, fear of being the target of another person's anger, fear of being embarrassed, fear of not being liked, fear that things will not turn out well, fear of not getting what we want, fear of being rejected, fear of being abandoned.

And this fear is probably not completely unfounded. Most of us will admit to having had experiences with conflict that turned out badly, that left us angry, disappointed, or not feeling very good about ourselves. Conflict that begins as a simple case of opposing positions can quickly spiral into an exchange of emotionally charged personal attacks. We may walk away from these moments wondering what just happened and where things went wrong. These are **destructive conflicts** and are characterized by verbal and nonverbal insults, ego attacks, inflexibility, a mindset of retaliation, and an exchange of negative emotion.[25] These conflicts are also known as **affective conflicts,** or **personalized conflicts,** because they are personal in nature and characterized by negative emotions, tension, personality clashes, and defensiveness. The outcome of these conflicts is often a damaged relationship.

Conflict Quote

Companies tend to be allergic to conflict— particularly companies that have been in operation for a long time. Being averse to conflict is understandable. Conflict is dangerous: It can damage relationships. It can threaten friendships. But conflict is the primary engine of creativity and innovation.
—Ronald Heifetz, Director of the Leadership Education Project at Harvard University's John F. Kennedy School of Government[26]

Our fears, however well-founded, are often misplaced. Conflict itself need not be feared, our real concern is the poor management of conflict that allows it to become destructive. In fact, since the 1960s, managers and social scientists have come to recognize the potentially positive aspects of conflict. Traditional views of conflict that blame troublemakers, emphasize legalistic forms of authority, and fail to recognize the importance of conflict have given way to the view that conflict is an integral part of change that can create opportunities for increased trust, relational growth, and joint problem solving. The focus on preventing conflict has given way to the notion that conflict can be *constructive* and there is an optimal level of conflict in an organization that is better than no conflict at all.[27] Constructive conflicts, also known as **cognitive conflicts**, or **substantive conflicts**, are characterized by arguments about facts, information, ideas, or plans. The benefits of optimal levels of **constructive conflict** include better decisions and innovative approaches to solving problems. The challenge is to manage the conflict so that it stays at an optimal level and is not handled in a dysfunctional way.[28] Table 1-2 lists the differences between destructive and constructive conflict.

Table 1- 2: Differences between Destructive and Constructive Conflict

Destructive Conflict	Constructive Conflict
Increases competition	Increases cooperation
Is mostly emotional	Is mostly cognitive
Involves personal attacks	Separates person and problem
Reduces outcome quality	Improves outcome quality
Doesn't solve problems	Solves problems
Weakens relationships	Strengthens relationships
Leads to hurtful behaviors	Leads to personal/professional growth

Conflict isn't a reflection of a dysfunctional relationship or emotional immaturity on the part of those involved. Healthy relationships will experience conflict. The difference between healthy and unhealthy relationships is not whether conflict exists, but how conflict is handled. Furthermore, not all conflicts can, or should, be resolved. In some cases, managing a conflict effectively is really the best that you can do.[29]

Conflict Quote

> *Conflict and disagreement offer wonderful opportunities to learn and grow. As long as you respect others' differences and things don't get personal, as long as you question the idea and not the person, then there will be room for discovery and movement toward the best solution.*
>
> —Matthew Gilbert, Communication Miracles at Work [30]

COMMUNICATION AND CONFLICT

While an informed view of conflict acknowledges that conflict can be a positive force, it also recognizes that in many cases that doesn't just *happen*. That outcome requires using the right tools to manage the process, and for this book, those are communication tools. This book employs a communication systems approach to understanding and managing conflict. It is through communication that conflict is initiated, expressed, maintained, escalated, and resolved. And lest you doubt the validity of this statement by recalling the last time you were angry with your coworker and didn't speak to him for a week, remember that not all communication is verbal. Your act of not speaking to your coworker will communicate plenty. Professor Linda Putnam of Texas A&M University conducts research on organizational conflict and negotiation. In her view, "Communication shapes the formation of issues, the emotional climate of conflicts, and the cyclical development of interaction." [31]

A communication systems approach to conflict views communication as a process that occurs within a system of interconnected elements and a conflict is simply an episode in the ongoing communication process. The elements in the system, as you might imagine, include the parties in the conflict, the messages exchanged between the parties, and the medium selected to deliver the messages. The entire

11

process occurs within a physical and psychological context. The physical context refers to characteristics of the actual physical setting, such as the size of the room, the arrangement of the chairs, and the noise level in the hallway. Psychological elements, such as the organizational culture, comprise the context or backdrop within which all communication takes place. Thus, each element in the system contributes to the meaning that is constructed by senders and interpreted by receivers.

A communication systems approach to conflict posits that the all the elements in the conflict system affect the conflict process. Thus, both the process and the outcomes can be changed by a change in any of the elements in the system.[32] If a sender is in a highly emotional state, communication will be affected. A conflict that occurs between people in a particular context, such as a private office, may be completely altered by changing the context to a dinner meeting with others present. If the integrity of a telephone message is compromised by static interference, the entire interaction is affected. If you are a party in a conflict, your personality, your mood, your experience and so forth, will affect the conflict process.

Consider this example. Imagine you're the last person working in your small office at the end of the day. You've finally finished the report that has caused you to work late and you print it. You look at the first page and see that you need a new ink cartridge for your printer – which you forgot to order. However, you know that your coworker and good buddy in the neighboring cubicle has an extra. You borrow it with the intent to order some the next day. This can turn out to be harmless decision on your part, or a pretty bad one depending on some aspects of the context. If your order of ink cartridges comes in before your buddy's printer runs out of ink, there's no problem. On the other hand, if the next morning your coworker has only a minute and a half to print out sales figures before heading to a meeting with the Vice President of Marketing, who abhors lateness, and he runs out of ink, reaches for his spare cartridge only to find it gone – he might have a problem with you. In this example one aspect of the context is changed, the coworker needs the cartridge or doesn't, and that affects the entire experience.

What's important here is the assertion that a change to one element in the conflict system will have an impact on the entire system. Consider, for example, how differently you respond to a conflict when you are in a great mood versus a bad mood, when you are under stress versus relaxed. In our example of the printer cartridges, imagine how differently you would respond to your coworker if he reacted to your action with a personal attack, "Keep your hands away from my desk, you selfish jerk" versus something a little less inflammatory. This is important because it means that, as parties in a conflict or the person responsible for helping others with conflict, we are able to create change in the conflict process by affecting the elements within the system.

Two implications follow. First is that the most effective approach for analyzing a conflict will be to consider the entire system and analyze how all the elements are contributing to the conflict and by considering which will be the easiest to impact. Consider this situation. Two departments are always at odds over the copier on the second floor, a resource they must share. Work is delayed and time is wasted as workers travel to the copier, only to find it in use. Two employees, one from each department, recently got into a heated argument when one arrived at the machine with an urgent job, only to find the other employee with an extremely large job already in progress and an unyielding attitude about interrupting the job. The discord between these employees grew and spread across their departments. A communication systems approach to this conflict would encourage us to look at all the elements involved in the conflict before deciding on the best approach for managing it. By doing that, we would easily be able to determine that having the quarreling employees sit down and talk out there differences would be much less effective than investing in an additional copier.

The second important implication from the assertions of the communication systems approach is that, since the messages exchanged between parties are elements in the system, conflicting parties engaged in conflict communication have the power to reshape the current interaction through what they say and do. New communication practices can change experiences and outcomes and can work to transform a negative experience into a positive one. Why is this important? Well, for one thing, it means that one individual can affect change in the conflict interaction. Managers who are caught in a destructive conflict can use different communication practices to shift to a constructive conflict. Perhaps even more important, this view means that a manager can effectively intervene in the destructive conflicts of others in the organization by creating change to an element in the system. Just the presence of a manager during an interaction can change the context of the interaction and thereby affect the entire system.[33]

As we saw in the example of the overworked copy machine, collaborative communication is not *always* the best way to manage or resolve every conflict. But when an issue is important and the relationship between the conflicting parties is valued, it usually will be. This book endeavors to provide you with an essential understanding of conflict, a framework for analyzing conflicts, and a working knowledge of the communication tools available for effective conflict management and resolution in the workplace. In this chapter, we introduce the basic concepts of conflict and communication, classic theories of conflict and their application to analyzing and addressing conflict. In Chapter 2, we'll discuss ways of analyzing conflict, and in Chapter 3, we'll explore techniques for working through conflict.

DEFINING CONFLICT

Conflict may be described in a number of ways. Dictionaries and management texts offer a range of synonyms: (1) to clash, disagree; (2) a battle or struggle; (3) antagonism or

14

opposition; (4) incompatibility or interference; (5) a mental struggle.[34]

Social scientists who study conflict often take a more detailed approach to the subject. Scientific literature offers these descriptions:

> *[C]onflict exists whenever incompatible activities occur.* (Deutsch, 1973)[35]

> *[Confict is] a situation in which interdependent people express (manifest or latent) differences in satisfying their individual needs and interests, and they experience interference from each other in accomplishing these goals.* (Donohue and Kolt, 1992)[36]

> *Conflict is the competition between interdependent parties who perceive that they have incompatible needs, goals, desires, or ideas.* (Van Slyke, 1999)[37]

> *Conflict is an expressed struggle between at least two interdependent parties who perceive incompatible goals, scarce resources, and interference from others in achieving their goals.* (Wilmot and Hocker, 2001)[38]

For our purposes, we will use the definition offered by Professor William Wilmot and professional mediator Joyce Hocker. Their definition includes the provision that a struggle between parties be expressed in order to be considered conflict. That expression, however, may not involve raised voices or flying objects. On the contrary, it may be nonverbal and quite subtle. In addition, the expression might not be directed toward the other person in the conflict. Frequently, conflicting parties will "vent" to a third party. Not every conflict requires direct, verbal acknowledgment between parties.

Wilmot and Hocker's definition also requires that conflicting parties be interdependent. **Interdependence** means that conflicting individuals are, in some important way, dependent on one another. The nature of interdependence varies across relationships. Sometimes interdependence is obvious, like the task interdependence that occurs when team members on a project team must use each other's expertise to compensate for each individual's gap in knowledge to get their work done. Sometimes, it's not so straightforward and direct, like when members from different organizations don't work together on any tasks, but may share the resources available in an office complex. Those shared resources create interdependence. Or when a company on the other side of the world shows no concern for the environment on the planet we all share.

Individuals or groups can be negatively interdependent, where a good outcome for one is at the expense of a good outcome for the other—one must sink for the other to swim. Alternatively, people or groups can be positively interdependent, meaning that all parties depend on each other for a positive or negative outcome that they will share. In other words, they will sink or swim together.

Conflict Quote

Interdependence is a central defining characteristic of work teams because team members, by virtue of their shared responsibility, are dependent upon one another.
—Anne Donnellon, Author of *Team Talk*[39]

GOALS

Another piece of the definition of conflict that warrants further explanation is the term "goals." Generally speaking, a goal is something that someone cares about. The intensity of conflict is related to how much the goals at the root of a conflict mean to the parties involved. There are numerous types of goals, including content goals, process goals, relational goals, identity goals, and values goals.[40]

1 CONTENT GOALS

Content goals involve our desires for the distribution of resources or the outcome of an event. Content goals might include such issues as who should receive a promotion, what should be done with an old storage room, or where the company should open a new office. Conflicts about content goals are the result of different ideas about what to do, where to go, who should get what, and the like. Conflicts over these goals almost always involve a perception of scarce resources. People want the same resource, but only one can have it; or they want different outcomes, but only one can happen.[41] For example, if two employees want to be promoted, but there is only one opening, or one partner thinks the new office should be in Dallas while another thinks that Houston is a better choice, content goals are at odds. Conflicts over content goals are very often among the easiest to resolve, although they can become genuinely heated when the goal is especially important to those involved.

Conflict over content goals can be low in intensity – You want Thai food for lunch and your lunch partner wants Mexican. However, conflicts over content goals can be extremely intense if the goals involved are enormously important to the parties involved – You think uprooting your family and moving to Minot, North Dakota so you can take that great job seems like an ideal plan, but your spouse disagrees.

2 PROCESS GOALS

Process goals are about how communication should happen. Conflicts over process goals occur when people do not agree on the type, amount, or depth of communication. In virtually every organization, there are many opportunities for conflict about communication processes and their outcomes.[42] For example, in some organizations the expression of differing opinions may be encouraged, while in others that sort of thing may be seen as inefficient or worse. Teams frequently encounter conflict over process goals if norms for processes are not explicitly discussed. Imagine a five member team.

17

Three members of the team happen to run into each other in the elevator, have a brief discussion, and make a quick decision about some matter. The remaining two members may think that decisions should be made through discussion with all team members. If so, they may have a conflict with the rest of the team over process goals.

Parties may not openly express their process goals in part because they assume that other people are using the same "process rulebook" as they are. However, this assumption may be in error. Think of times where your ideas of how things should proceed have differed from someone else's, and that came as a surprise. Students often cite dating as a good example of this because it can be awkward to ask about a person's dating rules on an initial date, so the students don't do it. Then they experience conflicts as they learn that they and their new dating partner have different rules for the process of dating. Complaints like, "He didn't call me after our date" or "She went out with someone else the next night," are common.

Conflict Quote

Brad Allen, who is Vice President for Corporate Communication and Investor Relations at Imation Corporation, acknowledges a personal dimension to organizational conflict. "Conflict at the interpersonal level," he says, "is frequently driven by style differences or personality differences. One conclusion I've drawn is that direct communication is best, but it must be within the right cultural context—

face-to-face, voice-to-voice. E-mail is not the way," he says. "Less mature people begin to feel empowered in an organization," says Allen, especially when they are somewhat removed from those they communicate with. His advice? "Quit the e-mail warfare, the one-upmanship. Walk over, call them, and resolve the issue." Don't let burgeoning egos or a desire to appear tough ruin a good business relationship.[43]

③ RELATIONAL GOALS

Relational goals involve how we want others to treat us and how we see our relationships with others. Unlike content goals, which are about something external to the conflicting parties, relational goals are psychological and can often arouse more emotion than content goals. Conflicts over these goals often involve differing expectations between the conflicting parties about their relationship. These conflicts may be about how things should be in the relationship or where the relationship should be going.[44]

Consider, for example, the case of a young woman named Lynn. She was a part-time instructor for a commuter college that served nontraditional students with an accelerated degree program. A newly hired campus director named Ann met with each of the instructors individually to introduce herself and to get to know them a little. After that initial meeting with Ann, Lynn chatted casually with her whenever she saw her in the hallway but made no special effort to seek her out for conversation. One day, Ann called Lynn into office for a meeting. She expressed disappointment and concern because Lynn didn't talk to her in the same friendly way that she did with students. Ann wondered if there was something wrong between them or if she had done something to keep them from becoming friends. Lynn, of course, was unsettled by the question. She

19

had always viewed her relationship with Ann as professional but not as a potential friendship. To Lynn, everything had been as it should be—until Ann questioned her about their relationship, which Lynn considered both inappropriate and strange. From that moment on, the relationship between the two women was strained on both sides. Ann and Lynn had different relational goals, with Ann wanting to be friends and with Lynn wanting something a bit different.

In this example, Ann has made her relational goals clear, but many times relational goals are unspoken, making it difficult for people to identify and work through the issues. These conflicts may be initiated or escalated by what one person reads into the words and actions of another and may continue for long periods because the concerns are not openly addressed. Not surprisingly, our relational goals frequently involve self-esteem issues and our interpretation of what other people tell us about our own self-worth.[45]

IDENTITY GOALS

Identity goals are also inextricably tied to our self-esteem. They are about who we believe we are and who other people perceive us to be. Our identities are what we believe to be true about ourselves and are intimately connected to our attitudes, values, and beliefs.[46] Our identity goals, then, can lead to conflict in a couple of ways. First, we may find ourselves in situations in which we feel that we are expected to act in a manner that we see as inconsistent with our identity. Second, we may find that others do not see us as we see ourselves. For example, most people typically don't want others to perceive them as foolish, immature, or weak, and when others do, conflict can result. Conflicts involving identity goals can be intensely emotional.

Identity goals and the desire to preserve and protect identity can become factors in a conflict, no matter how the conflict originally began. Often, we observe people in conflict dig into a losing position and refuse to yield, even when there is clear evidence that they should. They may cling to their position unless an alternative is presented that allows them to "save face" and yield without a threat to their identity. For example, suppose a process engineer considers his status as an expert in a certain area an important part of his identity. If a process he designed were to be improved by another engineer, he may reject the new design unless it's presented to him in a way that doesn't threaten his identity as an expert.

Even more often than relational goals, identity goals in a human interaction go unspoken. In fact, the participants in an interaction may not be consciously aware that they even have identity goals or that identity issues are providing fuel for an emotionally heated conflict.[47] Consider the story of Rob Peterson, who managed human resources for a software company. Rob was an achievement-oriented person who rarely ever sat still. He was always busy, working toward numerous personal and professional goals. Rob had been talking to his friend Sharon for a year about taking the PHR, a certification exam for human resource specialists. He frequently made statements that began with, "When I take the PHR," yet the study manuals for the exam sat in his office, untouched. One day when he made another reference to taking the exam, Sharon asked him if he really needed to take it. She pointed out that he had been talking about the exam for quite a while but was no closer to being ready for it. Since Rob considered himself to be achievement-oriented, ambitious, and organized, and Sharon's comment suggested that she didn't see him as any of those, it was a threat to his identity. Rob responded to Sharon by slipping into a bad mood but never speaking about the reason or discussing the identity issues related to her comment.

Identity goals can also lead to the avoidance of conflict in cases where the existence of conflict itself is perceived as a threat to our identity. This is most often likely for individuals who achieve much of their identity from a single source.[48] An employee, for example, who gains much of his identity—and thus his self-esteem—from having a "great attitude" about his job, may avoid expressing a conflict to his boss. If the conflict issue is serious and threatens the employee's satisfaction with his job, it can become a threat

21

to *who* the employee believes he is as a person, *how* he thinks others see him, and *what* he believes they value in him. With so much at stake, an employee with a vulnerable identity (one that is derived from a single source) is more likely to convince himself that everything is fine than face the threat of conflict.

Conflict Quote

> *When it comes to technical skill and the core competencies that make a company competitive, the ability to outperform others depends on the relationships of the people involved.* –Daniel Goleman [49]

 **VALUE GOALS**

Value goals are reflected in each of our other types of goals. Our values are what we think is important, right, or good. These values are reflected in our content, process, relational, and identity goals. However, they warrant mentioning separately because they are often at the root of deeply emotional conflicts that we can find confusing. We will sometimes discover ourselves intensely disliking people, not for something they have done *to us*, but for things they have done or the way they are in general. At times, we may be repelled by entire social groups because we perceive the groups to live by a different code than ourselves, one that violates our values. We may feel an undercurrent of conflict with people we have no obvious interdependence with, but their very nature and existence upsets us. How is this a goal? We have strong, deeply-rooted reasons for our values and can feel offended (or outraged) when we see others living and behaving in ways that are simply beyond the boundaries of what we think is fundamentally right.

MULTIPLE GOALS

Multiple goals can be at play in any conflict. Any combination of the five goals may appear in a conflict, and within any conflict, the various goals may differ in their relative importance. Goals can also change, develop, and fluctuate in relative importance during the course of conflict. In addition, some goals may be made explicit, while others remain implicit in a conflict.[50]

Keith Magnuson, a software sales manager who occasionally conducts training sessions for new clients, tells the story of arriving early on the day of a training session. Kelly, a training coordinator with the company for seven years, has the responsibility of preparing the training materials. On this particular day, Keith arrived at the office a little early, and the training materials were not yet ready. Rachel, Keith's assistant, had been with the company for just two years. She liked her job and her boss and considered Kelly to be a friend. Rachel was also in early that day and thought she could be helpful to Kelly and Keith by offering to assemble the materials. When Kelly arrived, she became very upset with Rachel for what she perceived as Rachel overstepping her role, and let her know it. Rachel then complained to Keith. In this conflict, the parties had different goals and the goals varied in importance. In Figures 1-1 and 1-2, we have diagrammed those goals, with font size representing the importance of the goal.

Figure 1-1   **Goals in Conflict: Kelly's Goals**

Kelly had been with the company for a while and was known to be someone who liked to retain control and to gain recognition for her experience and knowledge about the company. Her primary goal was probably her identity goal.

Identity Goal: I am the only one who can do my job well.

Process Goal: I should be asked before anyone does any of my work.

Relational Goal: Rachel should respect me.

Figure 1-2   **Goals in Conflict: Rachel's Goals**

Rachel was mostly interested in being a nice person and helping out two people she liked. What she was doing didn't matter to her much, so she may not have had important content or process goals.

Identity Goal: I'm a nice person.

Relational Goal: I want to help out.

The nature of the goals can affect the intensity of the conflict. Everyday, garden-variety conflicts may involve only content or process goals, but more serious conflicts usually feature at least one of the more ego-involving goals (that is, relational, identity, or values goals), even if these goals were not initially part of conflict. The presence of these goals, however, may be hidden behind more obvious and openly expressed content or process goals. A manager, for example, may make changes to an office procedure without discussing it with his assistant. The assistant may be adversely affected by the changes and—had she been consulted—may have been able to offer some suggestions on how to accomplish the manager's goals without all the negative consequences. The assistant may have a conflict

24

over the *content goal* of how the procedure should be written, as well as the *process goal* of not being consulted before changes are made in work she is intimately familiar with. In addition to these problems, the assistant may have conflict over the *relational goal* of having a relationship with her boss based on mutual respect and consideration, and an *identity goal* of being viewed as a valuable contributor of ideas. When and if she confronts her boss about these concerns, she may raise only the content and process goals, explicitly. The relational and identity goals, though, may be even more important to her because of her feelings about her boss and her satisfaction with her job.

LEVELS OF CONFLICT

Conflict occurs at various social levels and may include intergroup, intragroup, interpersonal, and intrapersonal levels. In this book we will focus on interpersonal conflicts. **Interpersonal conflict,** or conflict between two individuals, is a concern for many managers because of its frequency. These conflicts can occur between peers or between superiors and subordinates. They can occur between individuals in the same or different departments or even different organizations.[6] Much of the communication tools we discuss in this book are particularly useful for working through interpersonal conflicts.

Intergroup conflict refers to conflict between groups. The groups may be very large, such as nations, or much smaller social groups, such as the engineers or the production managers in a manufacturing facility. In organizations, intergroup conflicts can arise between groups at different levels in the organizational hierarchy (vertical conflict) or between groups at the same level (horizontal conflict). Intergroup conflict is often classified as institutionalized or non-institutionalized. Social institutions are shared ways of doing things. **Institutionalized conflict** is characterized by explicit rules for behavior that set boundaries between groups and legitimize differential treatment of individuals based on group membership.

Organizations that support differential treatment of group members—such as restrictions on specialized training or rules about dating clients or fellow employees—would be an example of a system that could lead to institutionalized conflict. In cases of **non-institutionalized conflict,** members of groups are sometimes treated differently because of their group membership, but the rules for this treatment are implicit and not viewed as legitimate.[52] In North American culture, racism in is an example of non-institutionalized conflict, and racial discrimination would be an example of differential treatment based on group membership that exists yet is not supported by formal social institutions.

Conflict Quote

While substantive conflict, if handled correctly, can be very productive, personalized conflict is almost never a good thing. There are several reasons. First, personalized conflict is fueled primarily by emotion (usually anger, frustration, and perceptions about someone else's personality, character, or motives).
　　—Robert Bacal, Institute for Conflict Prevention[51]

When conflict occurs between members of the same group, such as a conflict that occurs within a project team, it is known as **intragroup conflict** and is often about how problems should be solved and how scarce resources should be allocated. Intragroup conflicts are often categorized as task-oriented, process-oriented, or relationship-oriented. Task-oriented conflicts are cognitive in nature, are typically about the work at hand, and do not involve the personalities of the group members. Ironically, task-oriented conflict is the result of group members sharing diverse ideas, which is the very strength of group work. Moderate levels of task-oriented conflict are frequently associated with better outcomes for groups and are, therefore, considered desirable. Process-oriented conflicts, by contrast, are about how things should be done. Both process and relationship conflicts occur at lower levels than task conflict in high-performing teams during a project. And typically, teams that don't perform well tend to show higher levels of task and relationship conflict near project deadlines, suggesting that an approaching deadline may increase stress for teams that are underperforming.[53] Groups that perform well tend to discuss process and don't have to decide over and over how things should be done.

While moderate levels of task-oriented conflict are generally considered desirable for group work, this sort of conflict is clearly beneficial for some tasks and situations and not for others. Research shows that task-related conflict is often helpful with more complex tasks but not with routine tasks. Recent research further suggests that it is not simply the existence or amount of task conflict that improves group outcomes but, more importantly, it's how that conflict is handled. If group members use a constructive approach to their disagreements, then outcomes are improved, but they do not improve otherwise.[54]

In addition to conflict that individuals may experience with others, people can experience internal conflict, known as **intrapersonal conflict.** Like other levels of conflict, intrapersonal conflicts involve two competing desires or goals, but in this case the desires or goals are competing within the same person. Intrapersonal conflicts take one of several forms: approach-approach, approach-avoidance, and avoidance-avoidance.[55]

Approach-approach. An approach-approach conflict occurs when an individual is attracted to two desirable goals but cannot pursue both. As a simple example, imagine

27

choosing an item from a dessert menu and being torn between the chocolate brownie sundae and the strawberry cheesecake. You want only one dessert but are equally attracted to each of these items. Therefore, you have an approach-approach conflict in which you must choose between two attractive goals.

Approach-avoidance. In an approach-avoidance conflict, an individual is both attracted to and repelled by the same goal. In the preceding example, you could have an approach-avoidance conflict if you were on a diet yet wanted a dessert. Imagine you really want the chocolate brownie sundae, but your diet doesn't allow desserts. You are attracted to the dessert but repelled by the idea of sabotaging your diet.

Avoidance-avoidance. In the case of an avoidance-avoidance conflict, a person is faced with two equally undesirable alternatives. To illustrate this type of conflict, let's change our dessert example slightly. Imagine that you are invited to your boss's home for dinner. After dinner, strawberry cheesecake is served, but you are on a diet and trying to meet your goal of no desserts. In this situation, you have to choose between two undesirable alternatives. You can refuse the dessert, which may be perceived as rude by your boss, or you can eat the dessert and break your diet.

Of course, intrapersonal conflicts are often not as simple as any of the examples just described. Every day we encounter multiple approach or avoidance conflicts in which there are several alternatives, each with positive and negative aspects. As we face these conflicts, we often vacillate between alternatives and may have a difficult time making a choice and committing to it. In fact, any given conflict can become complex, developing at multiple levels. For example, if you know a colleague is acting unethically, you may experience interpersonal conflict with that colleague and intrapersonal conflict as you consider alternative actions to take.

Conflict Quote

A New York consulting executive acknowledges that conflict often occurs at more than one level simultaneously: "If it's purely a matter of finances, it's a fairly straightforward discussion," but usually there are underlying circumstances. "It's like the fight you have with your wife," he said. "At one level, it appears to be about that coat she bought but can't afford. And at another level, it's about something else." He paused for a moment and then added: "Look, no relationship lasts forever. You've got to invest in a relationship if it's going to work." That relationship may be personal or it may be professional, but if you want it to last, you may have to change the way you manage the conflict that occurs within it.[56]

THEORETICAL APPROACHES TO CONFLICT

A foundational theory for conflict is Realistic Conflict Theory, which simply states that conflict occurs when groups or individuals compete over scarce resources. But many other theories make valuable contributions to the understanding of how and why conflict happens and how to resolve it. Reading about theories can seem like boring down time to persons looking for practical tools to use in managing conflict, so we will not delve too deeply into the theoretical perspectives on conflict. We will take a brief look at a handful of theories that offer us a useful take away that we can apply later in our framework for analyzing conflict and our tools for working through conflict. [57]

Since we use a communication systems approach to conflict in this book, no one theory of those below offers perfect theoretical support for our approach. What you will see, though, is that a communication systems approach

29

allows us to pull the useful nuggets from each of these theories and use all of those pieces in our approach to analyzing and working through conflicts. The communication systems approach serves as an organizing framework for the pieces taken from each theory, whether the focus of the theory is the individual, the context, of the relationship between parties.

ATTRIBUTION THEORY

Attribution theory proposes that people are motivated to make sense of their social worlds so they produce explanations for behaviors that they observe in others and in themselves. Attributions can be **situational** (the behavior is caused by some aspect of the situation) or **dispositional** (the behavior is caused by some aspect of the person performing the behavior).[58] For example, if a co-worker is late to an important meeting with clients, we make a situational attribution if we assume that the cause of the co-worker's tardiness is particularly congested traffic along the co-worker's route to the office. Alternatively, we make a dispositional attribution if we think that the co-worker is late because she is unprofessional and doesn't value punctuality.

Research suggests that people tend to make dispositional attributions when explaining the behavior of others, despite information that highlights the importance of situational influences. This is known as the **fundamental attribution error**. In one study that demonstrates this phenomenon, spectators of a quiz show watched while people were assigned by the flip of a coin to the role of questioner or contestant. Those assigned the role of questioner were asked to produce ten difficult questions to ask the contestants. Not surprisingly, the questions reflected the individual questioner's personal store of knowledge, and so the contestants were able to answer only about 40 percent of the questions correctly. After observing the quiz show, spectators were asked to rate the general knowledge level of the questioner and contestant. Even though spectators were aware that roles were randomly assigned and the questions were created by the questioners (so, of course, they knew all the answers), they rated the questioners as having above average knowledge and the contestants as having below average knowledge.[59]

However, exceptions to this tendency to make dispositional attributions do occur. The first glaring exception is when we make attributions for our own behavior, especially if it's negative. We are very much aware of the situational factors that affect our own behavior, even if we tend not to way those heavily when making attributions about the behavior of others. If Sam is unprepared for a meeting, he's unreliable; if you are unprepared, it is because your computer crashed and your assistant has been out with the flu. This exception to the fundamental attribution error is known as the **actor-observer bias**.

Another exception to the tendency toward dispositional attributions occurs when we think that the person we're observing has no choice but to perform a particular behavior, or if the behavior is expected in a given situation.[60] For example, if an employee goes outside to smoke a cigarette because the company forbids smoking in the building, we wouldn't infer much about that employee because there is little choice about that behavior. If a supplier picks up the check for lunch with a buyer, we wouldn't attribute that behavior to generosity on the part of the supplier, because picking up the check would be expected in that situation.

As you might well imagine, the type of **causal attributions** that people make for another person's behavior have a tremendous impact on whether conflict will arise and whether or not it escalates or continues. If a colleague doesn't return a phone call or e-mail, we may think that he is rude and irresponsible—or we may think that he must be swamped with work. The explanations that we generate will have an effect on how we respond.

Attribution theory proposes that we observe behavior, make attributions about the causes for what we've seen, and then make inferences about the person performing the behavior. However, we rarely check our attributions and inferences for accuracy. A story shared from the early career years of a former employee of a West Coast bank illustrates this problem. Larry Morrison had been working in operations for two months when he was called into an unexpected meeting with his direct supervisor and the branch manager of his bank. The meeting was about his inability to meet report deadlines. Larry was responsible for preparing and submitting several reports daily, each by a certain time, and he had regularly missed the deadlines since he was hired. His boss was frustrated and felt that, after two months, Larry should be able to perform his job more effectively. She had the option to fire him because he was still in his ninety-day probationary period, but the quality of Larry's work was good, as was his attitude, so she opted to give him a warning and one more chance.

As soon as his boss expressed her concerns, Larry was able to resolve the issue. Until his supervisor voiced her concerns, Larry had no idea that his reports had specific deadlines throughout the day. The person who had trained Larry had done a wonderful job ensuring that he knew how to prepare the reports but never mentioned that they had to be submitted by any specific time. The two managers had inferred from Larry's behavior that he either lacked the ability or the motivation to perform his job effectively. That inference was incorrect, but no one checked on it for two months until the meeting, during which time Larry's performance was below expectations and his supervisor was growing increasingly frustrated. If the supervisor had checked the inference earlier, she could have spared herself a great deal of aggravation and saved the bank the inconvenience and expense incurred from the reports being submitted late.

Attribution theory offers us a few important take-aways we can apply to our efforts to manage our conflicts well and help our employees address their own conflicts more effectively. First, the awareness of the fundamental attribution error informs us that we should consciously pause and consider the situation factors that might have contributed to the behavior of another person, particularly behavior that has annoyed or offended us in some way.

Second, we should make the effort to confirm our attributions when important decisions or outcomes may be depending on them.

FIELD THEORY

Field theory proposes that each situation or context creates a psychological field with its own set of forces. The forces of a field will motivate some behaviors and inhibit others. Actual behavior is the result of the interaction between the person and the multiple forces present in the environment acting upon that person.[61] For example, the culture of one organization may consider competition among the sales force a value and demonstrate that value in many ways (e.g., bonuses, contests, awards, expressed expectations, etc.). Even within this sort of culture, other forces, such as friendships among the salespeople, may act to inhibit competition. The competitive behavior observed in any person will be the result of all the forces in the organizational field acting upon that person. In a different context that doesn't value competition, such as one's home, those same employees who exhibit competitive behavior may be extremely cooperative in response to the different forces in the environment. Field theory makes an important contribution to the study of conflict management in that it works against attribution errors by encouraging people to consider situational influences on behavior and conflict. Furthermore, field theory analysis encourages us to look at a specific goal and examine the driving and inhibiting factors. A useful outcome would be the recognition of inhibiting factors that we might be able to minimize or eliminate, or perhaps convert to driving forces. Take, for example, the goal of earning an "A" in a difficult class. Your friends might be an inhibiting factor because they may want you to socialize with them instead of study for your class. However, your friends could potentially be converted to driving forces if you asked them to encourage you and support your efforts.

SOCIAL EXCHANGE THEORY

Social exchange theory takes an economic approach to the understanding of relationships. Relationships are based on the exchange of benefits and costs. According to this theory, people are motivated to maximize rewards and minimize costs in relationships and make their choices according to that motivation. The benefits exchanged do no have to be in kind. For examples models and rock stars that date and marry are often exchanging benefits of different sorts. The models bring youth and beauty to the relationship and the rock stars bring money and an adventurous lifestyle. Relationships that provide more benefits with fewer costs will be more satisfying. Trouble comes when at least one person feels the costs of the relationship outweigh the benefits. A model might find the rock star lifestyle stressful after a while. A rock star might be less enthusiastic about a model after she's aged a little.

The expectations that people have for relationships, the alternatives they have to that relationship, and the investment that they have already made in it will also contribute to or detract from relational satisfaction and endurance. For example, imagine an employee who starts a new job finds that he enjoys it even more than he expected. He will experience job satisfaction. What happens, however, if he is offered another job that will pay more money than his current position? With this alternative as a comparison, he may experience less job satisfaction. However, if he feels that he has invested a significant amount of time and energy into learning his current job and building friendships with his co-workers, he may remain satisfied with his current job.[62]

EQUITY THEORY

Equity theory is a form of social exchange theory. For the work environment, it involves organizational justice or judgments about fairness in the organization. There are two primary concerns about fairness: one is about the way rewards are distributed, known as **distributive justice**, and the other is about the way things are done, known as

procedural justice. To ensure distributive justice, organizations and individual managers usually develop norms or rules about how rewards will be allocated. Rewards allocation rules in an organization can be based on equity, equality, or need.[63]

- **Equity-based allocation.** Rewards are distributed according to contribution. A greater reward is given to the person who works harder or contributes more. This is the standard for most North American organizations.
- **Equality-based allocation.** Rewards are distributed equally to all, regardless of contribution. Workmen's compensation is an example of this type of allocation. All employees are covered regardless of their work efforts or job title.
- **Need-based allocation.** Rewards are distributed on the basis of need. Certain grants for MBAs are examples of this type of reward. Only students with a demonstrated need are eligible for them.

Employees will also make judgments about whether the processes used for allocating resources or creating rules were fair and the procedures were correct. This is known as *procedural justice.* For example, an employee may wonder if, when making decisions about hiring, promotions, or compensation, managers are considering the appropriate criteria and ignoring inappropriate factors (e.g., age, race, or friendships).[64]

Conflict can result from the perception that resources are not being distributed justly or procedures for allocating resources are unfair. In work situations, perceived unfairness frequently results when employees do not receive the reward they expect. Employees perform a certain amount of work with the expectation that they will receive a certain amount of reward in return. Employee expectations about rewards can be based on previous experience or comparisons with others. In the mid-1990s, Mary Rodino, general manager of voice and data services for AT&T in Chicago, put together a star sales team that called on multi-million dollar clients that had left AT&T and tried to convince them to come back. The team was immensely successful at this difficult task and senior executives wanted to know why. They began looking into the team and found that their commission structure afforded its members more reward than corporate rules usually allowed. As this became known within the organization, sales reps in other divisions were upset and trouble began. The company decided it was time for restructuring. Mary's first thought was, "We've built this amazing team, and not only does the company not appreciate it, but this restructuring is going to destroy it." The team scaled back. Their commissions and bonuses were trimmed. Within a year, one-third of the team members no longer worked for AT&T and, before too long, neither did Mary.[65]

Equity exists when all employees perceive that their rewards are proportional to their contributions, especially as compared with other employees. Inequity exists when an employee feels that the rewards he or she is receiving are somehow different from those that other employees receive for the same amount of effort.[66]

Rewards for employees certainly include salary but also much more. Consider the case of two employees with the same job title, same salary, and same seniority level, but with one employee having a much larger office than the other. The employee with the smaller office may perceive the difference in office size as unjust treatment and become dissatisfied.

An interesting part of equity theory is the assertion that the inequity can be an over-benefit as well an under-benefit, and either of these alternatives will be distressing to the person who perceives it. In our example of the employees with large and small offices, the employee with the larger office may be just as uncomfortable with the arrangement as the employee with the smaller office, if she perceives her larger space as an over-benefit relative to the other employee.

PERSONALITY THEORIES AND PSYCHODYNAMIC THEORY

We are lumping psychodynamic theory and personality theories together, only because they focus primarily on the individual. There are two basic ways of theorizing about personality: Trait theories and type theories. Trait theorists are concerned with identifying individual characteristics and often with identifying and handful of traits that, combined, can be used to describe personality. The Big Five personality inventory is an example of a measure using this type of approach. The big five looks at five personality traits, like extroversion and consciousness, and tries to describe individual based on where they fall on the five traits. Type theorist, on the other hand, are typically interested in creating categories of personalities, or types, that people can be classified as. The Myers-Briggs Type Indicator is a commonly used example of a personality measure based on the type approach.

Within the two ways of thinking about personality, specific theories and personality assessments are plentiful and varied and are used in settings as diverse as career development offices, team building workshops, fashion magazines, and marital counseling cruises. What does that mean for us? Simply that understanding personality is something people find important. And this is not surprising. People frequently report a common source of conflict for them is personality conflict with a coworker. Often the coworker is perceived as having a "difficult" personality. In many cases, "difficult" basically means "different from mine."

For people trying to manage their own conflicts and particularly for managers helping employees with conflict, blaming personality for destructive conflict is not particularly helpful, and really an accurate assessment. If conflict is managed well, then personality should not be at the center of it. It might be a factor – it is easier to be forgiving of people we like – but we should not need to like someone's personality in order to be able to work with them.

We include psychodynamic theory here because it contributes something beyond the trait or type approach to our understanding of why people behave the way they do. Proponents of the **psychodynamic theory** rely heavily on the dynamic forces of the subconscious to explain the perceptions, emotions, and behaviors of individuals. These unconscious factors can lead people to behave in ways that are ineffective and even self-destructive. One familiar example of this behavior is *displacement*, in which a person experiencing a feeling toward an unsafe target turns that feeling toward a safe target. For instance, an employee is angry at her boss goes home. At the subconscious level, she doesn't feel comfortable being angry with him or expressing that anger because he is her boss. Displacement occurs when she goes home and begins arguing with her husband.[67] Alternatively, a manager who is having difficulty at home may take it out on employees. What is most useful about the psychodynamic theory for our purposes here is its assertion that sometimes conflicts are not about what they appear to be about on the surface.

Our brief discussion of personality is meant to encourage you to look outside of personality as a way of explaining and understanding conflict. Blaming personality makes it too easy to get destructive in the way we talk about conflict and makes it difficult for us to work through the conflict. (If you don't like someone's personality, what are you going to do, ask them to change it?) However, we do not intend to suggest that all personalities are created equal in terms of experiencing and working through conflict. If you took out a sheet of paper and on one side wrote down the ten personality characteristics you associate with a strong leader, and on the other side wrote down personality characteristics you think might lead an individual to experience more conflict, you might find traits appearing on both lists.

If you made another list of the personality traits that make it less likely that a person can work through conflict effectively. Defensiveness is a good example. If someone is high on defensiveness, they respond negatively to any criticism and typically refuse to take responsibility for their own actions, blaming other people and circumstances. As you can imagine, this makes it difficult to talk about behaviors that might need to change. The point is this: There are personality issues that can make dealing with another person difficult, but the personality excuse is often over used and should not be the default.

TRANSFORMATIONAL THEORY

In **transformational theory**, conflict is viewed as an important part of the development of relationships, organizations, and societies. Conflict occurs when there is a perceived discrepancy between how things actually are and how we think things should be, and through conflict progress is made toward how things should be. Conflict can initiate desired change and growth. A transformational approach to dealing with conflict doesn't focus on simply finding a solution to the immediate problem, but rather on examining underlying factors and relationships and determining how they are creating and being affected by conflict. The focus is on transforming relationships for long-term benefit.[68]

Food companies are introducing healthier products in response to concerns over consumer health issues, some of which have led to litigation and new labeling requirements. Fast-food restaurants such as McDonald's and Burger King have added more salads to their menus, while Hershey Foods Corporation has begun offering sugar-free versions of their most popular candies.[69] Kraft Foods and Unilever Best Foods North America are working to reduce or eliminate the trans fats from its favorite foods while preserving the taste.[70] These organizations are investing in long-term solutions to maintain and improve their relationship with consumers.

SYSTEMS THEORY

The **systems theory** follows that organizations are open, social systems composed of individuals engaged in patterned activities that are interdependent in the process of producing outputs. In general, open systems take resources from outside the system, transform them through the patterned activities of the system, and produce outputs, which are then exported to the environment. Organizations are made up of many subsystems. The organization as a whole and its subsystems refer to patterns of activities. The major components of social systems include their roles, norms, and values. **Roles** refer to the behaviors people are expected to perform when they occupy various positions in the system. **Norms** are the general expectations for how things should be done, and **values** are ideological in nature. These components ensure that activities will be repeated and patterns will develop.[71]

In organizational settings, systems are functional if they are performing or meeting organizational goals, but conflicts can occur and, if not managed well, can lead to systems to become dysfunctional. One part of the system may refuse to cooperate with another. A labor strike is a classic example. Alternatively, systems can become dysfunctional and that can lead to conflict. People in the system can get caught in a pattern of ineffective behavior and keep repeating the pattern, despite its ineffectiveness. Most of us who have worked in large organizations have dealt with dated, ineffective procedures that are slow to change and cause problems in the organization. Finally, breakdowns in a system can also occur when a part of the system claims too much power or increases expectations, causing instability.[72]

The communication systems approach allows us to incorporate a piece of each of these theories into our understanding of conflict by viewing the entire conflict system. For most managers, academic theories are only as good as their application to business problems. How can the theories we've described be useful to managers facing conflict in their organization? Each theory offers a different and valuable way of thinking about conflict. Each invites us to consider different aspects of the conflict system and ask different questions to help us understand it better (see Table 1-4).

Table 1-4: Practical Questions Suggested by Each Theory of Conflict

Theory	Questions
Attribution Theory	Are we making unwarranted inferences about an individual based on his or her behavior? What aspects of the situation could be contributing to the problem behavior?
Field Theory	Are there forces in our organizational environment that are encouraging problem behaviors? What forces are working against goal achievement? Can those forces be minimized, eliminated, or converted to driving forces?
Social Exchange and Equity Theory	Are rewards distributed fairly in our organization? Do we show bias or favoritism when we make decisions? Do employees perceive fairness or bias?
Psychodynamic Theory	Is there more at issue here than what there appears to be on the surface?
Transformational Theory	How can we make changes the will improve conditions, processes, outcomes, or long-term relationships?
Systems Theory	What are the identifiable elements and processes that are contributing to this conflict, and which can be changed?

Conflict Quote

In organizational systems, meaning-making can be conveyed and derived from language and images, stories and myths, conversational topics or themes, formal documents, acts, objects, rituals, and heroes, as well as orientation and training materials; all of these are created, sustained, and embedded in the formal and informal structure.

—Allan Church, Principal with W. Warner Burke Associates, Inc.[73]

COMMUNICATION AND CONFLICT

Organizations are open social systems composed of multiple subsystems, created through patterns of human interaction. When systems experience an episode of conflict, a change to any of the system's elements will affect the entire system. A communication systems approach to conflict allows us to consider any and all factors we are able to identify as contributors to the conflict and attempt to manage the conflict by creating an impact on an element in the system and thereby influencing the system. This might be a change to the context of the system, a change to a party in the system, or a change in the messages exchanged between the parties.

A communication systems approach to conflict suggests that changing the patterns of communication between the parties will affect the conflict itself. Some conflict is unavoidable, even in the best of relationships, and while communication cannot eliminate conflict, it certainly can work to transform it into a constructive, rather than destructive, experience. Systems can be durable and resist change. In addition, effective communication can be challenging in the best of circumstances. But in a heated

42

conflict where emotions are high, effective communication is even more difficult. Managers need to possess the skills to help them analyze conflict systems and choose the best strategy for managing or resolving conflict.

As you will discover in the remainder of this book, in most cases, a communication systems approach allows us to consider many options for the best way to deal with conflict, from changing aspects of the context, such as creating a new set of procedures, to using collaborative communication. We will see that when the relationship between the parties is important and the issue is of some consequence, collaborative communication will often produce to most desirable outcome. And managers who develop and employ the communication tools needed to manage conflict are more valuable to their organizations. In Chapter 2, we will show you how to analyze conflict using a communication systems approach, considering the important elements in the conflict system. In Chapter 3, we'll explore ways to use communication to work through conflicts and build relationships.

DISCUSSION QUESTIONS

1. Think of conflicts that you have experienced or witnessed in the past. Describe one that turned out to be a constructive conflict for the parties involved.

2. What are some metaphors for conflict not mentioned in the chapter? What do they reveal about your attitudes (and those of others) toward conflict? Create a positive personal metaphor for conflict.

3. Which type of goals do you think are the least likely to be made explicit? Why do you believe this is so? What do you think the effect of this would be on the resolution of conflicts with these goals?

4. Think of a recent conflict that you have experienced. Describe the nature of the goals underlying the conflict. How did that conflict end? Were all the goals discussed during the conflict, or did some remain implicit? If so, which ones?

5. Why do you think more serious conflicts usually involve relational or identity goals?

6. Analyze a recent conflict that you either participated in or witnessed. Which theories of conflict seemed to be involved? How did the conflict play itself out?

7. Recall a time from your own experience when you said something that you regretted saying. What do you think were the effects of what you said?

ENDNOTES

1. Robert D. Ramsey, "Peacekeeping in the Workplace: How to Handle Personality Clashes among Employees," *Supervision,* 58 (1997): 6.
2. Kenneth W. Thomas and W. H. Schmidt, "A Survey of Managerial Interests with Respect to Conflict," *Academy of Management Journal,* June 1, 1976.
3. Robert McNatt, "The List: Desk Rage," *BusinessWeek,* Monday, November 13, 2000, 12.
4. Daniel Costello, "Incidents of Desk Rage Disrupt America's Offices," *The Wall Street Journal,* January 16, 2001, B1, B4.
5. Ramsey, 7.
6. Clive Muir, "Can We All Get Along? The Interpersonal Challenge at Work," *Academy of Management Executive,* 14 (2000): 143–144.
7. Beth Nissen, "Overworked, Overwrought: 'Desk Rage' at Work," CNN.com, November 15, 2000.
8. Patricia Ruzich, "Triangles: Tools for Untangling Interpersonal Messes," *HR Magazine,* July 1999, 129.
9. Roger J. Volkema and Thomas J. Bergman, "Conflict Styles as Indicators of Behavioral Patterns in Interpersonal Conflicts," *The Journal of Social Psychology,* 135 (1995): 5–15.
10. Ramsey.
11. Daniel Dana, "The Dana Measure of Financial Cost of Organizational Conflict." Available: http://www.mediationworks.com, 2001.
12. Roger J. Volkema and Thomas J. Bergmann, "Conflict Styles as Indicators of Behavioral Patterns in Interpersonal Conflicts." *The Journal of Social Psychology,* Vol. 135 (1995): 5–15.
13. Volkema and Bergmann, 5–15.

14. Daniel Dana, *Conflict Resolution* (New York: McGraw-Hill, 2001).
15. Volkema and Bergmann.
16. Pamela R. Johnson and Julie Indvik, "Rudeness at Work: Impulse over Restraint." *Public Personnel Management,* 30 (2001): 457–465.
17. Muir.
18. Carol Elliott, "Safety Policies Can Limit Violence in the Workplace," *South Bend Tribune,* April 7, 2002, B1, B3.
19. Johnson and Indvik.
20. Jennifer Daw, "Road Rage, Air Rage, and Now Desk Rage," *APA Monitor on Psychology,* July/August (2001): 52–54.
21. Nissen
22. Ibid.
23. Ramsey.
24. Ibid.
25. Wilmot and Hocker.
26. William C. Taylor, "The Leader of the Future," *Fast Company,* June 1999. Available: http://www .fastcompany.com/online/25/heifetz.html.
27. Joe Kelly, "Make Conflict Work for You," *Harvard Business Review,* 48 (1970): 103–113.
28. M. Afzalur Rahim, *Managing Conflict in Organizations,* 2nd ed. (Westport, CT: Praeger, 1992).
29. Beebe, Beebe, and Redmond.
30. Matthew Gilbert, *Communication Miracles at Work* (Berkeley, CA: Canari Press, 2002), 228.
31. Linda L. Putnam, "Communication and Interpersonal Conflict in Organizations," *Management Communication Quarterly,* 1 (1988): 295.
32. Steven A. Beebe, Susan J. Beebe, and Mark V. Redmond, *Interpersonal Communication: Relating to Others* (Boston: Allyn and Bacon, 1999).
33. Stephen W. Littlejohn and Kathy Domenici, *Engaging Communication in Conflict* (Thousand Oaks, CA: Sage, 2001).
34. *Webster's Desk Dictionary* (New York: Random House, 1993), 94.
35. M. Deutch, "Conflicts: Productive and Destructive," in *Conflict Resolution Through Communication,* edited by F. E. Jandt (New York: Harper & Row, 1973), 156.
36. W. A. Donohue and R. Kolt, *Managing Interpersonal Conflict* (Newbury Park, CA: Sage, 1992), 3.

37. Erik J. Van Slyke, *Listening to Conflict: Finding Constructive Solutions to Workplace Disputes* (New York: Amacom, 1999), 5.
38. William W. Wilmot and Joyce L. Hocker, *Interpersonal Conflict,* 6th ed. (New York: McGraw-Hill Higher Education, 2001), 41.
39. Anne Donnellon, *Team Talk: The Power of Language in Team Dynamics* (Boston: Harvard Business School Press, 1996), 33.
40. Wilmot and Hocker.
41. Ibid.
42. Ibid.
43. Brad Allen, Imation Corporation, telephone interview, Oakdale, MN, March 3, 2003.
44. Wilmot and Hocker.
45. Douglas Stone, Bruce Patton, and Sheila Heen, *Difficult Conversations* (New York: Viking, 1999).
46. Stone, Patton, and Heen.
47. Ibid.
48. Wilmot and Hocker.
49. Daniel Goleman, *Working with Emotional Intelligence* (New York: Bantam Books, 1998), 299.
50. William W. Wilmot and Joyce L. Hocker, *Interpersonal Conflict,* 6th ed. (New York: McGraw-Hill Higher Education, 2001), 41.
51. Robert Bacal, "Conflict and Cooperation in the Workplace," 1998. Available at Institute for Conflict Prevention web site, http://www.work911.com/articles.htm.
52. M. Afzalur Rahim, *Managing Conflict in Organizations,* 2nd ed. (Westport, CT: Praeger, 1992).
53. Karen A. Jehn and Elizabeth A. Mannix, "The Dynamic Nature of Conflict: A Longitudinal Study of Intragroup Conflict and Group Performance," *Academy of Management Journal,* 44 (2001): 238–251.
54. Leslie A. DeChurch and Michelle A. Marks, "Maximizing the Benefits of Task Conflict: The Role of Conflict Management," *The International Journal of Conflict Management,* 12 (2001): 4–22.
55. Kurt Lewin, *A Dynamic Theory of Personality* (New York: McGraw-Hill, 1935).
56. Telephone interview, New York, NY, February 28, 2003.
57. Myra Warren Isenhart and Michael Spangle, *Collaborative Approaches to Resolving Conflict* (Thousand Oaks, CA: Sage, 2000), 4–10.

58. Fritz Heider, *The Psychology of Interpersonal Relations* (New York: Wiley, 1958).

59. Lee Ross, "The Intuitive Psychologist and His Shortcomings: Distortions in the Attribution Process," in *Advances in Experimental Social Psychology*, vol. 10, edited by L. Berkowitz (New York: Academic Press, 1977), 174–221.

60. Edward Jones and Keith Davis, "A Theory of Correspondent Inference: From Acts to Dispositions," in *Advances in Experimental Social Psychology*, vol. 2, edited by L. Berkowitz (New York: Academic Press, 1965), 219–266.

61. Kurt Lewin, *Field Theory in Social Science* (New York: Harper, 1951).

62. Sharon S. Brehm, *Intimate Relationships* (New York: McGraw-Hill, 1992), 157–171.

63. John M. Levine and Leigh Thompson, "Conflict in Groups," in *Social Psychology: Handbook of Basic Principles,* edited by E. Tory Higgins and Arie W. Kruglanski (New York: Guilford Press, 1996), 745–776.

64. Levine and Thompson.

65. Cheryl Dahle, "Don't Get Mad—Get over It!" *Fast Company,* vol. 22, February 1999, 190.

66. E. Walster, E. Berscheid, and G. W. Walster, "New Directions in Equity Research," *Journal of Personality and Social Psychology*, 25 (1973): 151–176.

67. Isenhart and Spangle.

68. Ibid.

69. Sarah Ellison and Brian Steinberg, "To Eat, or Not to Eat," *The Wall Street Journal,* Friday, June 20, 2003, B1.

70. Leila Abboud, "The Truth about Trans Fats: Coming to a Label Near You," *The Wall Street Journal,* Thursday, July 10, 2003, D1.

71. Daniel Katz and Robert Kahn, *The Social Psychology of Organizations* (New York: Wiley, 1966).

72. Isenhart and Spangle.

73. Allan H. Church, "The Character of Organizational Communication: A Review and New Conceptualization," *The International Journal of Organizational Analysis,* 2 (1994): 18–53.

CHAPTER

2

ANALYZING CONFLICTS

Conflicts can be confusing to the parties involved and to those observing them. When people are angry or hurt, they often don't understand exactly what's happening in a conflict, let alone know how to resolve it. In fact, people commonly act in ways that make a conflict worse and encourage others to repeat the very behaviors that upset them in the first place. Consider, if you will, a manager who rants and raves whenever he receives bad news from his production supervisor. Furthermore, he complains that his supervisor keeps him in the dark and won't tell him what's going wrong until it's too late to stop it.

Much of our difficulty in understanding conflicts stems from a traditionally employed method of analyzing them, which is *finding fault* and *affixing blame,* or the "who screwed up analysis." In our preceding example, the manager fails to recognize that he contributes to a lack of upward communication by his volatile reactions. Instead, he sees his supervisor as the problem. But conflict is rarely about a "bad guy" who does bad things, so laying blame isn't an effective strategy for conflict analysis. Labeling one person as "the problem" is a counterproductive measure that inhibits any real problem solving. Once someone is given the label, that person becomes the only one with the power to make a change. Others may try to fix "the problem," but no one can *make* another person change. And it's unlikely that "the problem" will agree that all of the fault lies with him and be both motivated and ready to change, or agree to be "fixed" by the others in the conflict.[1]

Instead of rooting out the problem person, the communication systems approach, as described in Chapter 1, encourages analyzing the conflict as a system. This analysis means determining each of the elements in the conflict and how they work together, evaluating individual contributions, identifying dysfunctional patterns, and exploring what purpose the conflict serves within the system. Because a change to any part of the system will create change in the rest, a communication systems approach expands a manager's options for dealing with conflict. Rather than fixing a problem individual, a manager can try a variety of strategies that target different elements in the conflict, such as changing the context or changing the messages that are sent.[2]

This approach will work best when accompanied by a general change in our motivation from finding ways to blame someone who has "screwed up" and make them motivated enough to change (typically by making them feel bad in some way), to helping everyone, including someone who has done something we don't agree with perform at his or her best.

In order to deal effectively with conflict, whether it be their own or that of their employees, managers need a framework to organize their analysis of the factors that may be contributing to the problem and guide their choice of an appropriate course of action to resolve or manage the conflict. An analysis of conflict using the communication systems approach begins with identifying the issues, much like any other type of analysis, but from there, instead of looking for the "screw up" the analysis looks at the physical and psychological context, the primary parties involved and other parties who may be affecting the conflict system, and the messages exchanged between the parties. The analysis seeks to identify anything that is contributing to the conflict. Managers may discover, after a thorough examination of a conflict, that it can be resolved easily without involving the conflicting parties—by procuring more resources or changing a policy, for example. If a manager decides that a conflict issue must be raised with the conflicting parties, preparing by analyzing the conflict before bringing the issue up will make the resolution process go smoother.

In this chapter, we'll discuss various factors that can contribute to conflict. For any given conflict it would be virtually impossible to identify each and every contributing factor, but fortunately that isn't necessary to work through a conflict effectively. We'll look at common contributing factors that are characteristics associated with the various elements of the conflict communication system. The elements include the physical and psychological context of the conflict, the conflicting parties, and the messages and the feedback exchanged between the parties. We also consider various properties of these elements (see Table 2-1), that are commonly associated with conflict, such as the conflict management styles of the parties or a highly stressful context.

Table 2-1: Elements of the Conflict System and Some of their Properties

Parties	Physical/Psychological Context	Messages/Feedback
Level of conflict Personalities Conflict management styles	Stress Policies, procedures, norms Power distribution Trust	Verbal aggression Ineffective tactics Nonverbal cues Defensiveness

Conflict Quote

According to Kristen Bihary, most organizational conflict is either interpersonal or conceptual in nature. Bihary is vice president for corporate communication at Eaton Corporation, a $7.2 billion diversified industrial manufacturer headquartered in Cleveland, Ohio. She claims, "People put forward competing concepts or ideas, and, if the organization does not specifically understand how to manage conflict, others will react personally rather than professionally or intellectually to what is being proposed."

"Conflict can also arise as a result of the disruption caused by change," she says. Frequently, says Bihary, acquisitions and mergers will cause the greatest stress in an organization as it tries to establish a single culture for all employees.

Avoiding conflict, in her view, is not a good idea. "You don't get anywhere by holding back or holding in." Many organizations, according to Bihary, are really passive/aggressive in nature. The reason? "Many people don't like confrontation. They don't like telling other people 'no.' You think you have agreement on an issue or course of action and head off in that direction," she says. "Later you find out you didn't have agreement at all. The result is inefficiency at best and disaster at worst."[3]

FACTORS CONTRIBUTING TO CONFLICT IN THE WORKPLACE

Numerous factors contribute to conflict in the workplace. Some are very specific to certain industries, organizations, groups, or individuals, while some are common to all workplace situations. In this section, we will discuss contributing factors that are present in work environments across all industries and organizations.

PHYSICAL AND PSYCHOLOGICAL CONTEXT FACTORS

Structural factors are situational. They exist apart from the individuals who are exposed to them, and they tend to affect most people in similar ways. As we noted in Chapter 1, the contribution of situational factors is often undervalued when we attempt to explain people's behavior. When we analyze conflicts, we must be cautious about committing this attribution error. Sometimes conflict is rooted in situational factors. At times, the conflict can be resolved by changing the situation, without ever bringing the conflicting parties together or raising the issue with either of them. Each conflict will present its own unique, situational variables for us to consider as we analyze the problem. For now, we'll review just a handful of the most common situational contributors to conflict.

STRESS

Without question, the number one contributor to conflict in the workplace today is work-related **stress**. One in every ten U.S. workers considers job stress a major problem, and 30 percent of Americans actually lose sleep from work-related stress.[4] Stress is a psychological and physiological reaction to what we perceive to be a threat in our environment. A common source of stress today is the need to accomplish many tasks in a short period of time. Phil, a controller, shares an example. As an accountant, he is responsible for preparing numerous monthly reports during a limited time span. Periodically, he experiences a great deal of stress as he tries to complete the reports while dealing with repeated interruptions that distract him from the task. The threat he faces is not completing his reports by the time his supervisor needs them.

A certain amount of stress or pressure, like that from an approaching deadline, is often what energizes people to get things done. The problem with stress is that the human response to it hasn't changed over time, even though the demands of our environment have. We still respond to stress with the fight-or-flight reaction, which may have been appropriate when the threats we faced were wild animals or raiding marauders, but it is not particularly useful for the kinds of stressful situations we typically encounter today, like a tight deadline or a crashed computer (or even worse – these two co-occurring!). In stressful situations, we continue to have a physical response, but today's situations usually require a mental solution. While we do occasionally see people respond to an unresponsive computer by hitting it or to an uncooperative vending machine by kicking it, those reactions are usually ineffective for coping with our workplace stressors.

Conflict Quote

Stress is one of many potential triggers for aggressive responses in the workplace.
—Susan Burroughs, Roosevelt University[5]

Though these physical outbursts aren't really effective, the stress response releases chemicals into our systems to prepare us for physical activity. Frequently experiencing the stress response without any corresponding physical exertion can lead to serious health problems that can be costly to an organization. While stress related problems such as headaches, fatigue, hypertension, and heart disease can be expensive for an organization, for our purposes, another important consequence of stress is just as concerning. That is the effect stress has on our ability to communicate well. The stress induced irritability or short fuse that is so pervasive in today's workforce is a major contributor to workplace conflict.

What are the causes of stress in the workplace? If you have worked at all in the last decade, then you already know. While people react differently to any given environment, and some people may experience more stress than others, certain aspects of the modern workplace tend to cause most people to experience stress.

- **Workload.** At one time, "multitasking" was not a commonly used word. Now it's a goal to which most of us aspire. People continually try to do more in less time and to get more done in a day. Much of the increase in workload is related to improved communication technologies and the resulting glut of incoming information that many experience at work. A survey of 1,200 workers of a variety of sorts found employees receiving an average of 200 messages a day when all media are included (i.e., e-mail, phone, memo, letter, etc.).[6] People are often faced with more work than they can complete during regular work hours. As many as 52 percent of North American workers put in more than 12 hours a day and 50 percent regularly skip lunch so they can complete their work.[7] Workload issues can be especially problematic for those who are not fitted well with their job and perhaps can't work as efficiently as others do or don't enjoy their work as much.
- **Social environment.** The social climate in the workplace can be a source of stress in many ways. In an environment that doesn't provide support for work-related issues or personal and family issues, a closed communication culture, a hostile environment, or an extremely competitive environment all can be stressful. Workplace romances that fail can also be a source of stress. More than half of human resource professionals report that workplace romances have had a negative impact on their organizations.[8]
- **Physical environment.** Aspects of the physical environment, such as loud noise, poor air circulation, or excessive heat can add to stress levels. An important

recent development in offices in cities across the country is crowding. More employees are being squeezed into smaller spaces, often by creating cubicles from partitions that allow for little privacy. Sean Hutchinson, president of the New York–based Integra Realty Resources, Inc., calls it the "scrunch factor." According to Hutchinson, "The big guys take offices that are just as big or bigger than in the past, while the minions are getting stuffed into smaller and smaller spaces."[9] Social psychologists have long known that putting more people into smaller spaces can cause negative effects. In one study, researchers put ten people into an 8-by-12 foot room and ten people into a 20-by-30 foot room and then took some physical and psychological measurements. The people in the smaller room had higher blood pressure and heart rates than those in the larger room and made more errors on difficult mental tasks.[10]

· **Concerns over job.** Especially in tough economic times and in the industries most affected by them, people may experience concern over job security. Fear of downsizing can be distracting and stressful. In addition, eliminating jobs means those remaining must absorb more responsibilities, contributing to work overload. This stress can be reduced or alleviated to some degree by clear communication from management about the future and by allowing employees to participate in decision making to the extent possible.

Conflict Quote

One of every eight workers works in a cubicle—and they show higher stress levels.
—Sean Hutchinson, President, Integra Realty Resources[11]

POLICIES, PROCEDURES, AND NORMS

The written and unwritten rules in organizations can create a culture that encourages and even rewards conflict. A culture that creates excessive competition will create conflict as well. For example, organizations may have contests and prizes that encourage unnecessary competition and inhibit cooperation. Competition encourages employees to work harder for their own reward. It does not make them better employees, nor does it encourage them to have pride in their work. One survey of 1,200 employees at three different companies found that offering performance incentive pay actually de-motivated the majority of employees. In 1990, Rob Rodin ended the incentive programs at Marshall Industries, an electronics distributor based in El Monte, California. Over the next six years, employee turnover dropped by 85 percent, while sales grew from $565 million to $1.7 billion. "By paying well but knocking out pep rallies, contests, prizes, commissions, and individual bonuses, we became more collaborative and adaptable," says Rodin.[12]

In some organizations the procedures that employees are required to follow are not well thought out or have not changed with the changing needs of the organization and cause strife between employees. At one Midwestern plastics plant, maintenance technicians had the responsibility of maintaining and repairing three large blow-molding machines. When they needed parts, they wrote a note on a scrap of paper and handed it to the purchasing clerk. If the slips contained complete information, the clerk would type a purchase order and have it signed by the purchasing manager before the order could be placed. If the scrap of paper didn't include the necessary ordering information, the purchasing clerk had to wander around the production floor looking for a mechanic to get more details. When the clerk didn't have time for this, incomplete orders would be set aside. These cumbersome procedures made the process of getting a part annoyingly slow, so that when the items arrived, the impatient mechanics would take the parts from the dock before the receiving paperwork was completed. This procedure created problems later when the invoice for the part came in but purchasing would have no record of the part arriving.

Conflict Quote

> *The idea of merit rating is alluring, but the effect is exactly the opposite of what the words promise. Everyone propels himself forward, or tries to, for his own good, for his own life preserver. The organization is the loser.*
>
> —W. Edwards Deming[13]

Several conflicts arose from these procedures. The purchasing clerk was often frustrated by orders with incomplete information and felt the mechanics were uncooperative. The mechanics were irritated with purchasing because it seemed to take so long to get parts. And accounting wasn't happy with purchasing because they had invoices they couldn't process.

The real problem wasn't any department or person but poorly considered procedures. An external consultant was hired to review the efficiency of the purchasing department and made significant improvements in the process of ordering repair and maintenance items. Mechanics were required to place orders by handwriting purchase orders, including part numbers, and placing the order in an inbox for purchasing. If the order was incomplete, it was returned to the mechanic via the mechanic's inbox. The receiving area was locked, so no items could be removed without being properly accounted for. The simple changes in procedures made the process more efficient and reduced the conflict. But note that it took someone spending the time to consider what wasn't working in the system, and someone with sufficient power in the organization to implement a change.

Organizations often contribute to conflict among employees in other ways, as well. Unclear job descriptions and ambiguous lines of authority create confusion and frustration. Managers who transfer or promote difficult employees just to be rid of them simply spread dysfunction instead of rewarding worthy employees. Similarly, as equity theory suggests, managers who attempt to quiet complainers or troublemakers by giving them what they want can create a perception of social injustice among employees. Organizational policies or procedures can also create difficulties for people external to the organization, such as impersonal policies that prevent employees from satisfying customer needs or voice-mail systems that require callers to navigate their way through a maze of messages.

DIVERSITY

As we make achieving diversity a goal, we are often surprised by the challenges we encounter when we bring people with different ways of doing things together. Brian, Associate Director of Admissions for the highly ranked MBA program, shared a story about a newly arrived Middle Eastern student. Brian's first meeting with the student had gone quite well—until the very end. As the meeting was finishing, Brian noticed a marked change in the student's demeanor. The student was visibly upset and Brian was confused. He asked the student if he had done something to offend him. The student replied that he had. As their meeting had come to an end, Brian had relaxed into his chair and crossed his legs, resting his ankle across his knee. In doing so he exposed the bottom of his shoe to the student, a profoundly offensive act in the student's native culture.

As we become a global economy, cultural diversity will become an increasingly critical factor in organizational success. Achieving diversity, however, is only part of the goal. While the recommendations in this book are based on conflicts in Western culture, the importance of learning how to work through conflict with people who are from diverse cultural backgrounds is undeniable.

Conflict Quote

Diversity is not some vague, idealistic concept. The face of the workforce is changing, and, like it or not, here we come. Smart companies get it. Enlightened corporations know it's good for workers and good for the bottom line.

MANAGING CONFLICT IN THE WORKPLACE

—Alexis Herman, United States Secretary of
Labor, 1997–2001[14]

Culture refers to the shared values, beliefs, norms, language, and social institutions that guide everyday life for a group of people. Cultures vary in innumerable ways but a few major and important dimensions are worthy of your attention. Cultures can be individualist or collectivist. This dimension reflects the degree to which individuals value their connection with the group versus their independence as individuals. Individualist cultures value independence over the group, whereas collectivist cultures place the group above the individual. The United States, Canada, and Western Europe are individualist cultures, while Asian and South American countries tend to be collectivist. Individualist and collectivist cultures approach conflict very differently. Collectivists often avoid conflict, preferring to maintain harmony and save "face." Individualists, on the other hand, don't enjoy conflict, certainly, but are much less likely to avoid it.[15]

Cultures also vary in communication styles. In some cultures, communication is very direct, while in others the style is indirect. In cultures featuring an indirect style, it is expected that relational exchanges will come before getting down to business. As a result, direct communication may be perceived as rude. Cultures with indirect styles of communication also tend to be highly context-dependent, wherein a great deal of the meaning of a message is derived from the context of the communication (who's in the room, what time of day we're meeting, where the exchange takes place, and so on). In some cultures, the style of communication is very expressive and animated, while in other cultures it is more reserved.[16]

Cultures may also differ in their interpretation of time. Some cultures value multitasking, while others prefer doing one thing at a time. Some cultures value punctuality, while others do not. These differences can become a problem when they are misinterpreted. An indirect style of

59

communication can seem like disorganization to someone who is accustomed to a more direct, "get down to business" style. And a lack of concern for punctuality can be interpreted as a lack of consideration and professionalism. Learning about other cultures and managing expectations is crucial to preventing this type of misinterpretation.[17]

There are many ways to think about diversity in the workplace. Typically, when we refer to diversity we mean gender, racial, or ethnic diversity. But even people that look the same, share a common religion, and hail from the same place can hold very different attitudes, values, and beliefs. If you have siblings, then you know that even people who share some genetic material and have grown up in similar environments can vehemently disagree about a whole host of items.

FACTORS RELATED TO THE PARTIES

CONFLICT MANAGEMENT STYLES

No discussion of conflict management would be complete without discussing styles of conflict management. Conflict management style refers to the preferred way an individual responds to conflict. Most style theorists do not suggest that a person responds to all conflict in a certain way, but rather that people have a preferred way of responding that they will use if factors do not influence them to use another style.

Numerous typologies have been proposed to classify ways of responding, from a dichotomy of cooperation and competition to more recent complex two-dimensional grids that produce five styles (see Table 2-2). Two of these models seem to be most popular. In one, the dimensions of the grid represent the *degree of concern* for self and the degree of concern for others when responding to conflict. In the other, the dimensions represent *levels of cooperation* and *levels of aggressiveness.* Both models produce a similar collection of five styles: avoiding, obliging or accommodating, dominating or competing, integrating or collaborating, and compromising.[18]

Table 2-2 **Conflict Management Styles**

Conflict management styles result from the combination of the degree of concern an individual has for one's self, or aggressiveness, and the degree of concern an individual has for the other, or cooperation, when responding to conflict.

Concern for Self or "Aggressiveness"	Concern for Others or "Cooperation"	Conflict Handling Style
Low	Low	Avoiding
Low	High	Obliging/Accommodating
High	Low	Dominating/Competing
High	High	Integrating/Collaborating
Moderate	Moderate	Compromising

An **avoiding style** is characterized by a desire to avoid confrontation, disagreements, and unpleasant exchanges with others. There are times when, due to situational factors, each of us might decide that we are better off not expressing conflict. Perhaps the issue is not important enough to us (I'd rather have Italian for lunch, but you want Mexican), or perhaps the relationship is not very important, desirable, or enduring (the temporary receptionist keeps mispronouncing your name). In some cases, the costs of confrontation can be too high, for example, if an issue is raised with a superior in the organization who may respond negatively. At times, we may avoid conflict for the benefit of the other party. (This person can't handle this information right now.) But when people prefer to avoid conflict regardless of situational factors, and they use various strategies to maintain avoidance, they are demonstrating an avoiding style of conflict management.[20]

You can avoid conflict in a number of ways. A common technique is withdrawal or refusal to participate in the conflict. Avoidance can also be achieved by denying that a problem exists or claiming that resolution of the conflict is hopeless, so participating in the conflict is pointless.

Intimidating someone else so that an issue is never raised is another time-tested way to avoid a conflict.

When people employ an avoidant style, conflicts can escalate because they aren't being resolved or managed. The other party may be unaware of the nature of the conflict because it hasn't been expressed directly, so members of the party may unwittingly engage in behaviors that exacerbate the problem. When the other party *is* aware of the problem, failure to raise an issue may be perceived as a lack of concern or interest. Although the avoiding parties are unlikely to directly express the conflict to the other party, they are likely to talk about it to others in the organization. This, too, can lead to escalation as the parties being avoided may discover they are being talked about "behind their backs."[20]

Avoiding conflict can lead to more avoidance. Because of the tendency for avoidance to escalate conflict, conflicts that have been avoided may eventually grow to the point where they simply must be confronted. Often this need for confrontation occurs after negative emotions have festered, our worst thoughts about the other party have been confirmed, and many third parties have been made aware of the situation. At this point, it may be even more difficult for parties to handle the confrontation well, which can end up confirming the negative expectations about conflict that kept the avoiding person from raising the issue in the first place and can ultimately lead to more avoidance.[21]

The **obliging** or **accommodating style** is characterized by a preference for cooperation, a willingness to make concessions, and by giving in to the wishes of others. The accommodating style puts harmony between parties ahead of individual needs and interests, which is a useful strategy in some situations, such as when an issue is very important to one person but not to the other. In certain situations we all accommodate or oblige. For example, we may feel that the other party in a conflict has more power and that accommodation is the only alternative.[47]

Sometimes when people accommodate, they say "yes" when they would rather say "no" because they feel the need to be compassionate or to avoid hurting someone. However, people who frequently give in for the good of others may accommodate or oblige resentfully. They may become complainers, play the martyr, or give in when there is no compelling reason, simply to demonstrate how nice they are.[23]

Accommodators often don't recognize that it is possible to refuse someone compassionately. People who have a difficult time saying no often don't place as much importance on their own feelings as they do on the feelings of others. But they can learn communication skills that allow them to express an understanding of the other person's feelings without ignoring their own, thus making it easier for them to stand their ground. They often need to learn that it's okay to have boundaries and limits.[24]

In contrast to the agreeableness of the accommodating style, the **dominating** or **competing style** of conflict management is confrontational and characterized by a win/lose mindset. Those who use this style like to argue their position but, if that isn't working, will use their power or authority to get their way. Individuals who prefer this style are more interested in winning the conflict than in reaching a solution that satisfies both parties. In fact, for some the "win" must be at the expense of the other party to be truly satisfying. This lack of concern for the other party is evident in this style by a tendency toward put-downs and personal attacks. This style can often lead to destructive conflict as parties engage in an exchange of insults, verbal abuse, and threats.[25]

However, the dominating or competing style isn't always destructive, and, in some cases, it may be the most appropriate style. A person's role may require a dominating or competing style. In a courtroom, for example, lawyers compete. In organizations, managers are sometimes required to make decisions and give directions that will not be well received but are unavoidable, such as when an organization is downsizing.[26]

The **integrating** or **collaborating style** is most effective when the option to negotiate for a mutually satisfying outcome exists. This style seeks creative and innovative win/win solutions to problems. In addition, the collaborative processes themselves can build relationships. This style clearly demands more energy and time than the others, so it may not always be the best choice. It is the appropriate strategy when both parties care about the goals and the relationship.[27]

Successful collaboration is accomplished through communication. Collaborative communication tools help parties understand each other's perspective, making it possible for both parties to work toward creating mutually satisfying solutions. We'll look more closely at collaborative communication techniques in Chapter 3.

The **compromising style** seeks the middle ground. Each party gives a little and gets a little. Sometimes compromising is the best strategy. For example, a compromise can yield fair results with little time invested when an issue is not terribly important. But compromising means that no one gets exactly what he or she wants. So compromising doesn't necessarily result in parties who are satisfied with the results of the resolution. Each party may have to give up something important. Compromise is often a default strategy that circumvents true problem solving and doesn't allow parties to realize the benefits of conflict.[28]

Though people may have a preference for one style of response to conflict, they can and do use different styles in different situations. For example, in organizational settings, employees are more likely to be accommodating or obliging with the boss. Recent research shows that, rather than relying solely on one style for a given conflict, people typically use a pattern of styles. They may strategically switch styles as they notice the one they are using isn't working.[29]

Despite our ability to use many styles, we may tend habitually to overuse one conflict management style across many diverse situations, whether that style is most appropriate or not. Managers can make the most out of learning about conflict management styles by recognizing which styles are most effective in different situations and by making sure they and their employees are competent in using each of the styles. Being flexible in the style used is crucial to successful management and resolution of conflict. Examples of situations in which each of these styles is most appropriate are given in Table 2-3. Note that some of these situations could be moments in an ongoing conflict; the style choice for that moment would represent one style used in a pattern of styles.[30]

Conflict management style is a product of the parties' communication. Attending to communication can reveal to parties and observers what styles the parties are using. It is important to note that style does not result simply from the intention to use a particular style. For example, a party may intend to be integrating but may be perceived as competing due to ineffective communication.[31] Table 2-3 provides examples of communication indicators of the different styles.

PERSONALITY

Many conflicts are rooted in **personality** clashes. Different personalities produce different ideas about what and how things should be done. This very diversity is what many organizations strive to achieve in their workforce so they can benefit from decision making and problem solving done with varied perspectives and expertise. Research on teamwork suggests that diverse teams do produce better solutions to complex problems, but it takes them a little bit longer to get there. Most organizations seem to believe the benefits are worth the extra effort.

Table 2-3 Communication Indicators and Various Situations in which a Particular Conflict Management Style may be Appropriate

Style	Situations in Which Each Style is Appropriate	Communication Indicators of Style
Avoiding	• The issue is unimportant. • The relationship is unimportant. • One or both of the parties needs a "time-out" from the conflict. • The risk of confronting outweighs the potential benefits significantly.	Avoiding communication seeks to deny or dismiss the conflict, make a joke of it, or change the subject. • "I don't want to talk about it." • "Everyone gets in a bad mood occasionally." • "How 'bout them Cubs?"
Obliging or Accommodating	• A requirement for competition is part of your role. • You are making an unpopular decision from a position of authority. • Others do not have the resources to make a good decision.	Obliging or accommodating communication yields to the other party. • "It's up to you. Whatever you want is fine with me." • "I don't care."
Dominating or Competing	• Time is available. • The issue is important. • The relationship is	Dominating or competing seeks to persuade or force the other party to change

	important. • Parties are willing and able to participate in problem solving. • Having all parties involved will improve the quality of the solution.	positions and to control the other party. • "You're being ridiculous." • "Oh yeah, that's a really *great* [sarcastically] idea." • "That's your responsibility, not mine."
Integrating or Collaborating	• Time is available. • The issue is important. • The relationship is important. • Parties are willing and able to participate in problem solving. • Having all parties involved will improve the quality of the solution.	Integrating or collaborating focuses on reaching an understanding of the different parties' perspectives and working toward a solution that satisfies each party's interests. • "When you said that, did you mean... ?" • "I can see how that would be upsetting to you." • "I can do more of that."
Compromising	• Other styles have been tried and failed. • Quick, temporary solution is needed. • Parties are equally powerful and goals are mutually exclusive.	Compromising communication attempts to work out a fair solution. • "If you're willing to do without this, I'll be willing to do without that." • "I'll do it today, if you do it tomorrow."

Understanding the nature of personality can help managers and employees view individual differences in a more positive way. People think about personality in terms of types and traits. **Traits** are enduring characteristics that individuals display, and **personality types** are categories of personalities that share a collection of traits. People with different personality types, who share few common traits, may have difficulty seeing eye-to-eye. This difficulty can lead to destructive conflict if we make negative inferences about the other's behaviors. Consider the situation of Li and Brad, two very different personalities who were members of an MBA team working to prepare a marketing plan for a new business. At the very first team meeting, Li produced a timeline for the creation of the marketing plan. He had divided the project into smaller tasks, arranged them in sequence, and assigned a deadline for each task. At the next team meeting, he distributed the timeline and wanted to assign members of the team to the different tasks. Li saw this as a way to help the team get off to a good start, but Brad didn't share that view. He saw the timeline as premature and restricting. Brad felt that some tasks would require more research than others, and he wanted to have plenty of time to explore any relevant information. Furthermore, he thought Li was acting overly controlling and that preparing a timeline without input from the rest of the team was inappropriate.

Clashes of personality such as this one can lead to personal attacks and quickly spiral out of control. But diversity among personalities doesn't have to result in destructive conflict if people can learn to value differences and recognize how they contribute to better outcomes. In the preceding example, the team valued working together and learned how to appreciate the contributions that each member made. In the end, Brad recognized that Li's schedule helped keep them on track, and Li remained flexible enough to skip a task in the sequence on his timeline because more information was desired.

Still, we've all encountered what we would call "difficult people." Were those experiences just the result of our inability to tolerate diversity or our lack of effective communication skills? Probably neither. Research shows that there are, indeed, some personalities that are more prone to destructive conflict than others. For example, people who are highly authoritarian have a tendency to judge others by a rigid set of moral standards; to identify with high-status individuals; and to reject, criticize, and punish low-status individuals. Closely related is dogmatism. Dogmatic individuals are close-minded and inflexible, with very little tolerance for other points of view. Individuals high in either of these characteristics can be difficult to work with and for.[32]

Individuals high in codependence can also create challenges for workplace relations. Codependent individuals have difficulty keeping a healthy psychological distance between themselves and others. They feel the need to control the behavior of others and are not able to detach themselves appropriately from the consequences of the behaviors of others. Codependent people usually have low levels of trust. They tend to hoard information as something to be controlled. They also operate from the mindset that there are never enough resources to go around. They hide their feelings and let them simmer under the façade of feeling what is expected of them, and they may experience low self-esteem or be terribly upset when things change. Such people tend to take things very personally and have difficulty separating accountability from blame. As you can well imagine, these people can be difficult to work with, and the combination of behavioral tendencies associated with codependence is particularly unfortunate for effective conflict management. Not only do codependent individuals fail to communicate openly, it is difficult for others to communicate openly with them because they are so easily offended.[33]

Conflict Quote

An employee with an attitude problem is a manager's nightmare. When the problem is an entitlement mentality—evidenced by rolling eyeballs, sighs, and antagonistic body language—it can drive managers crazy because stopping such "silent" behavior is difficult when employees so easily can deny there's a problem.
—Paul Facone, Director of Employment and Development, Paramount Pictures[34]

RELATIONSHIP FACTORS

Any analysis should include an examination of the relationship between the parties. Communication between people creates a history that the people carry with them. The history, the patterns of communication, will shape expectations about future interactions and will influence how they turn out. Two aspects of the relationship are considered here: power and trust. Each has a profound effect on the communication of the parties and, therefore, their ability to effectively implement a communication approach to working through conflicts.

POWER

Power is about perceptions of control over others or the ability to influence others in some way. Power isn't something that is just "out there." It's a property of a relationship and results from the dependence of one person on another for the achievement of a goal. The amount of perceived power is affected by the importance of the goal and the alternatives for achieving the goal without depending on the powerful person.

Positions of power are created by people's needs and wants. If you have something that nobody wants, you don't have much power. But if you can help people get what they

70

want or prevent them from getting what they want, you are in a powerful position. A now-classic way to think about power identifies five sources of power: legitimate power, reward power, coercive power, expert power, and referent power. **Legitimate power** comes from the authority assigned to a position that a person holds. Managers and supervisors have legitimate power over their direct reports. But people in organizations also develop power through resources, relationships, and expertise. If you have control over the distribution or withholding of valuable resources, you have **reward power** and can influence the behavior of those who depend on you for those resources. Conversely, if you have the ability to punish others in some way and can control them, you have **coercive power.** If you have valuable information, know the answers, or can solve a problem, you have some measure of **expert power.** If you are well liked and people want to be liked by you, or if you have qualities that are socially appealing such as good persuasive speaking skills, you have a certain amount of influence over others through **referent power.** 35

most dangerous ➚

When conflicts develop, the power distribution in a relationship suddenly becomes more important. But who has power in a conflict is not always clear. Conflict makes people emotional, and when emotions are high, people often feel helpless and may underestimate just how much power they have. William Wilmot and Joyce Hocker, in their book on interpersonal conflict, offer this rule of thumb: Each party in a conflict will always believe that the other party has more power.36

Managers dealing with conflict should carefully analyze the power structures of the conflicting parties. Sometimes this is difficult because not only do the conflicting parties have low levels of confidence in their own power, but also communication between conflicting parties may not always reveal the true power dynamics. People can talk about what they did or what they decided without necessarily mentioning the people who influenced them. For example, Juan may be upset with Jennifer for not supporting an idea in a meeting. When asked to explain, Jennifer may not say that

71

the referent power of Lonnie, who also failed to support the idea, was an influencing factor, but may instead simply cite some problems with the idea.[37]

Sometimes power issues are themselves at the root of a conflict. People may feel that others are trying to gain power over them, which they choose to reject. Comments such as these reveal this sort of thinking:

- You're just trying to control me.
- You can't tell me what to do.
- You're not my boss.
- Who do you think you are?
- What makes you think you have the right to... ?

Power affects the choices people make when they respond to conflict. In situations in which conflict occurs between parties with higher and lower levels of power, the party with lower power may feel that the options available are limited. Formal grievance procedures offer employees an opportunity to be heard in these situations. In the absence of this alternative, or if this alternative has proven ineffective in the past, employees may resort to withholding information, complaining to others, calling in sick, making mistakes, and other indirect responses. As Wilmot and Hocker point out, power corrupts, but so does powerlessness.[38]

In addition to ensuring that an effective grievance process is in place, what can managers do to help employees deal with this type of situation more effectively? The main goal is to balance the perception of power somewhat. Empowering employees is an effort to achieve that sense of balance and increase employees' feelings of control. Organizations empower their employees in a number of ways. Organizational hierarchies can be flattened; managers can use a more participative leadership style; and impersonalized forms of power, such as rules or regulations, can be put in place, reducing the perceived personalized power of those with higher levels of power.[39]

Conflicts between higher- and lower-status employees may be especially common during times of change. A good manager creates and guides change and also considers how changes in the organization will affect employees, not just in the tasks they perform but also how they feel. Managers can empower their employees during times of change by letting them participate in the process and by emphasizing a "we" approach in the organization. Employees who feel that their needs have been considered will also feel that they are valued as employees and will be more supportive of change.

Conflict Quote

As a general rule, it makes sense to use power only as a last resort. When you use power you win and the other loses. More often than not, resentment and alienation accompany this action.

—John Ford, Mediation Training Institute[40]

Conflict in organizations is not limited to parties of unequal power. Parties of equal power may have interdependency through shared resources or reliance on each other to complete tasks. When in conflict, these parties often engage in win/lose bargaining strategies that escalate conflict rather than resolve it and negatively affect the functioning of the organization. The conflicting parties may be unable to clearly communicate with each other. Task-interdependent departments may fail to coordinate their efforts effectively and may argue over who is supposed to do what. One party may attempt to strengthen its position in the organization by denigrating others, and those who share important resources may begin to demand their own.[41]

Managers can help in this situation by clearly assigning roles, promoting a culture of teamwork, and attaching efforts to outcomes. They can reduce interdependency between parties or, alternatively, increase it to the point where parties can't risk the conflict. They may take measures to strengthen the relationships within the organization and to improve the attitudes employees have toward the organization. Of course, even with these efforts, conflicts will occur. To be ready for them, organizations can train employees to communicate effectively and to negotiate so they can manage most conflicts on their own. For more serious conflicts, managers can establish a central figure to regulate or arbitrate conflicts in order to protect the organization from business problems.[42]

TRUST

In organizations, trust occurs at different levels. At the organizational level, trust occurs within the organizational system and between the system and the environment. Unethical practices in an organization have a devastating effect on trust, both internal and external to the organization. WorldCom and Enron are well-known examples of organizations that lost trust at a macro level through unethical actions.

Within the organization, trust, or the lack of it, is part of an organization's culture. The structure of an organization, its written policies, and unspoken norms work to create and communicate the presence or absence of trust. Flatter structures and employee empowerment communicate the organization's trust in its employees and can, in turn, engender employee trust in the organization. The words and actions of individual managers can also engender trust. Managers who say what they mean and do what they say they will are trusted.

Trust in organizations can take a variety of forms.[43]

- **Trust in ability.** For managers and employees alike, it's important to trust in the ability of others to do their job. Micromanaging is an expression of lack of trust in employees.
- **Trust in a commitment to the relationship.** Managers want to know that employees are going to stay with the organization, and employees want to feel that their jobs are secure. In difficult economic times, when

74

downsizing is a popular survival strategy for organizations, trust in relational commitment suffers.

· **Trust in the other's concern for your welfare.** At work and in other areas of our lives, we are suspicious of people who do not seem to have our best interest at heart.

· **Trust in another's regard for privileged information.** In organizations, managers and employees must be able to trust that disclosed confidential information will not be shared with others or be used against the discloser.

Conflict Quote

Integrity—acting openly, honestly, and consistently—sets apart outstanding performers in jobs of every kind. Take those in sales roles that depend on the strength of ongoing relationships. In such a job, someone who hides crucial information, breaks promises, or fails to fulfill commitments undermines the trust so vital to repeat business.

—Daniel Goleman, Author of *Working with Emotional Intelligence* [44]

The existence of trust is important for working through conflicts constructively because it affects the process in several ways. Working through conflicts collaboratively requires sharing information. Parties must be willing to share their interests and goals with each other in order to discover what really matters. But as we just saw, information can be a source of power. Parties must trust that the information they share will not be used against them in some way. They must believe that the others at the table will work for a mutually satisfying solution to a problem and not resort to using force or threats to get the best solution for themselves. Trust must be present for conflicting parties to communicate openly with each other about their interests.

Trust and open communication are also required for building relationships through collaborative processes. However, relationship building may not always be required or even desired in every conflict situation. The simplicity of the parties' goals and the degree and duration of interdependency may make it more or less desirable to develop the relationship. For example, parties in conflict over a single transaction are interdependent but only until the transaction is completed and so may not be concerned with real relationship building. In that case, they could reach a useful agreement without really trusting each other.

When relationships are important, parties can build trust by being courteous, sincere, fair, and not losing control. Over time, trust develops when all parties are honest, reliable, and competent.[45] Other behaviors that promote trust include appropriate self-disclosure. Revealing small amounts of appropriate information communicates trust. When this disclosure is reciprocated and repeated, trust grows. Communication behaviors that demonstrate acceptance, such as listening attentively, asking questions to clarify understanding, and giving affirming feedback also help build trust.[46]

MESSAGES AND FEEDBACK: WHEN COMMUNICATION MAKES IT WORSE

This book posits the idea that the most effective way to work through conflict is by engaging conflicting parties in the communication process. But conflicts are not simply resolved through communication. They are initiated, maintained, and escalated through communication, as well. Managers can use the messages exchanged between parties to diagnose whether a conflict is constructive or destructive. If the messages reveal a task-oriented, cognitive conflict, a manager may wisely decide to let it be. However, if conflict messages contain ego attacks and abusive language, action on the part of the manager may be required.

Abusive language, or verbal aggression, uses words to injure another person's self-concept. This aggression may include insults, character judgments, and hurtful comments, such as "You're an idiot" or "Why don't you do us all a favor and quit?" Abusive language tends to be vague ("You're such a loser") and ineffective at creating change. Yet some people when confronted with conflict immediately resort to the strategy of attacking another person's character. Some who frequently use this strategy think many of their comments are genuinely humorous. Others, however, don't see them that way and find verbal aggressors less credible and without as many legitimate arguments as those who refrain from verbal aggression. Furthermore, in the workplace, if a higher-status person ridicules a lower-status person's mode of speech or clothing, or negatively labels him or her (e.g., whiner, screw-up), it may be considered harassment.[47]

Look at the following examples of verbal aggression:

· You are completely incompetent.
· Did you dress with the lights off this morning?
· You talk like a first-grader.
· You have absolutely no class.

Other communication techniques that can escalate a conflict, or at the minimum stall any chance of resolution, include:[48]

· **Mindreading.** In a conflict, we often think we know more than we really do about the other party and why they've done what they have done. We may *tell* them why they did something or what they were thinking, rather than asking them. And the motives and thoughts we imagine to be true are typically negative.
· **Self-summarizing.** When people self-summarize, they keep repeating what they have already said. They communicate no new information, but what's worse is that they ignore the responses of the other party.
· **Cross-complaining.** When parties cross-complain, they each are sharing complaints and no one is listening. "You've been late to our team meetings three times this

week." "And *you've* forgotten to post the minutes to the web site."

- **Kitchen-sinking.** Conflicts can escalate when the parties bring up more and more issues and throw "everything but the kitchen sink" into the conflict.

Of course, not all communication comes from words. In fact, some anthropologists think that only about 7 percent of the meaning of a message is derived from the verbal content.[49] The rest is nonverbal. Nonverbal communication is important in all of our face-to-face interactions, but it's a critical aspect of conflict communication. Nonverbal communication is vitally important to the communication of our attitudes and emotions and in helping others know how to interpret our verbal message. The same words accompanied by a smile have a very different meaning when yelled and accompanied by a clenched fist.

The meaning of most nonverbal cues is culture-based, but certain facial expressions (anger is one of them) are recognized across cultures. In Western culture, we communicate an interest in what someone else is saying through making eye contact, leaning toward the person, and showing facial expressions. We can just as easily communicate that we don't agree with another person and even that we don't value or respect that person through our nonverbal communication. A listener who rolls her eyes, crosses her arms, looks away, slouches down in her seat, shakes her head "no" continually, and wears a rejecting scowl on her face is communicating more than "I don't agree with the point you're making." She's also communicating that "I don't care about the point you're making *and* I don't care about you." These nonverbal messages can make collaborative communication between parties all but impossible and can be so frustrating that they actually escalate conflict.

LEVEL OF CONFLICT AS A FACTOR IN THE SYSTEM

In Chapter 1, we discussed the different social levels at which conflict can occur. At each level of conflict, factors unique to that level can contribute to the conflict and should be considered in your analysis.

INTRAPERSONAL FACTORS

A specific form of intrapersonal conflict frequently experienced in the workplace is known as role conflict. A *role* is the collection of behaviors and attitudes commonly expected from someone who occupies a particular social position.[50] For example, a receptionist has a social role. We expect a receptionist to be friendly, efficient, and have good phone manners. Teacher, CEO, administrative assistant, mother, and priest are all examples of social roles. Each of us occupies numerous social roles and, as a result, can experience role conflict. A role **conflict** occurs when the expectations for one role clash with the expectations for another.[51] For example, a commonly experienced form of role conflict occurs when people seek to balance work and family life. A working parent with a sick child may experience role conflict because the expectation for the parent role would be to stay home and care for the sick child, but the expectation for the employee role would be to go to work. Many organizations understand this sort of role conflict and create policies to assist their employees to manage it; such policies can greatly reduce the amount of stress and internal conflict experienced by literally everyone in the organization.

Managers also can help employees avoid experiencing intrapersonal conflict by periodically assessing employee-job fit. Employees can experience intrapersonal conflict if they are asked to perform tasks for which they are not adequately prepared, or if they are expected to do more than they can accomplish. Furthermore, they can experience conflict if their own goals are at odds with the goals of their department or organization. Some organizations actually encourage intrapersonal conflict through conflicting goals and policies and unclear expectations.[52]

INTERPERSONAL FACTORS

Interpersonal conflicts are quite common in organizations and can be particularly perplexing for mid-level managers.[53] For conflicts that occur at the interpersonal level, the nature of the relationship between the parties is the most important factor to analyze. In organizations, as was previously noted, differences in status will have an effect on how conflicts are likely to be expressed. But interpersonal relationships are defined by much more than positions in an organizational hierarchy.

Interpersonal conflicts are often influenced by a strong relationship history. These can be difficult to analyze from the outside. A remark or behavior that seems perfectly innocent to an outsider may be laden with meaning to the conflicting parties. Part of the relationship history can include patterns that are associated with recurring conflict. Patterns may emerge in the way that the conflict begins, the response of the parties, and the outcomes. Analyzing these patterns can be the first step in preventing the conflict from reoccurring.

Consider, if you will, an administrative assistant who has been in the same position for several years. Because the office has been reorganized, she no longer works for the person who hired her but now has several bosses and frequently finds herself in conflict with one in particular. The new boss tends to overcommit himself, get behind in his work, and then demand that the assistant invest extra time in getting her projects done at the expense of her other bosses or personal time. When the boss takes on another project, the assistant knows what's coming, but she never raises the issue because she feels that, since the reorganization, her job may be in jeopardy. Instead, she becomes unpleasant and complains to anyone who will listen. After a while, the pattern is familiar and frustrating to her and really annoying to those who must listen to her complaints.

After a while, this sort of microevent can be fairly easy to recognize. Even the parties involved know the pattern but may be unable to see how they are contributing to its continuance. Managers investigating these conflicts can begin by asking questions about how they are initiated, who responds and how, and what would happen if the conflict went away. They may explore the possibility that the conflict serves some function for the system.[54]

INTERGROUP FACTORS

Intergroup conflict is possible anytime there are two or more clearly delineated groups in an organization. The groups we are part of are called **ingroups,** and the groups to which we do not belong are called **outgroups.** We develop part of our identity from our group memberships. We are democrats, we are Catholics, we are Americans, and we are parents. All of these memberships mean something to us and contribute to our identity. Similarly, in organizations, we gain part of our identity from the groups we claim as ours. We are part of the marketing department. We are the plastics division. We are plant 16. We are the first shift.

Because we derive part of our identity from our social groups, we are motivated to see those groups in a positive light. In fact, we are motivated to view them more positively than other groups. After all, if another group was better than our own, wouldn't we be a member of that group instead? Favoring your own group is called *ingroup bias.* Research shows that even when people know that they are part of a group that has been created by randomly assigning group membership to one of two groups, they believe the group they are part of is better than the other group.[55]

Not only do people show this almost automatic favoritism toward their own groups, they can be equally motivated to see outgroups unfavorably. People often contribute to the positive perception of their own group by denigrating outgroups. They tend to show more cooperation with their ingroup and more competition with the outgroup. In addition, people tend to view their ingroup as being heterogeneous, while viewing the outgroup as being "all alike."[56]

Conflict Quote

We define [diversity] as any collective mixture characterized by differences and similarities. That definition takes into consideration race and gender, plus behavioral diversity. A lot of times, you think you have diversity representation because a lot of individuals in a room look different, or they may have different educational experiences, geographic locations, or differences of origin. But, if you have invited all of these people into the room expecting them to assimilate into the environment, then you have diversity representation without true diversity.

—Melanie L. Harrington, Executive Director, American Institute for Managing Diversity, Inc.[57]

Once people develop a negative perception about an outgroup, the perception can be difficult to change. When people believe something about a social group, they tend to be more attentive to behaviors from group members that confirm their belief and less attentive to disconfirming behaviors. Similarly, people tend to jump to conclusions about correlations between something observed in one member of a group and the group as a whole. For example, let's say that in your organization your ingroup is "nonsmokers" and the outgroup is "smokers." You observe someone you know to be a smoker throwing a candy wrapper on the floor in the break-room. Furthermore, you notice that outside around the company picnic table where some people eat their lunch in the summer, there are numerous cigarette butts. You may conclude that smokers are slobs. The fact may be that one or two smokers litter and the rest don't. And it may be that an equal percentage of nonsmokers also litter. But because of ingroup bias, you are more likely to notice the littering of a smoker and more likely to believe that all smokers are litterbugs. The habit of littering then becomes another point of differentiation between your group and the outgroup, making a positive attitude toward the outgroup even less likely to develop.

A negative attitude toward a group or members of a group because of their group membership is a form of prejudice. Prejudice (or *judging before knowing*) is associated with beliefs about a social group that contribute to the negative evaluation of its members. The collection of beliefs we hold about a social group is called a stereotype. Stereotyping, you may recall, is attributing to all members of a group or class those characteristics or behaviors observed in just one or a few. Although we tend to think of stereotypes as negative ("Overweight people are lazy"), they can be positive as well ("Overweight people are jolly"). But all stereotypes generalize beliefs across a social group and are commonly used to make hasty, often negative, judgments about members of an outgroup.

A popular example of intergroup conflict in organizations is the line and staff conflict. In an organization, the line generally refers to the production department, although in a non-manufacturing facility, the customer service–oriented workers could be considered the line. The staff refers to the non-management employees who support the line, such as human resources or quality control. These groups often have different goals within the organization. Line workers generally focus on aspects of the daily operations of the organization while staff workers may have more long-range goals. These groups also frequently have different backgrounds and values.[58]

Organizations can contribute to conflict between line and staff by enhancing the perception of status differences through matters of distributive justice. For instance, one organization created three separate classes of employees: management, clerical, and production. Management employees were salaried, while clerical and production workers were paid hourly. Although their hourly wages were similar, the clerical and production employees were very distinct groups with an undercurrent of conflict between them. In part, this conflict resulted from issues of distributive justice. In some cases, what might be perceived as an unfair distribution of rewards simply couldn't be avoided. For example, the production area was hot, noisy, and smelled like chemicals, while the staff offices were climate-controlled and quiet. However, the organization contributed to the feelings of division between the groups in other ways. For example, production employees ate lunch in a dingy break-room, while clerical employees were permitted to eat in a plush conference room. Production employees had to punch the clock, while clerical employees were permitted to handwrite their time cards.

Just as organizations can help create conflict between groups, they can help prevent it as well. Establishing superordinate goals is one way to foster cooperation in place of competition. A **superordinate goal** is one that cannot be achieved without the participation of both groups. In order to be effective, the goal must be one that both groups will benefit from achieving. In a now-famous study, Muzafer Sherif looked first at the effects of competition over scarce resources and then at the effects of superordinate goals on two groups of 11-year-old boys. Twenty-two boys from Oklahoma City were invited to a Boy Scouts of America camp that was surrounded by Robbers Cave State Park. The groups of boys arrived in two different buses on different days and for a while were unaware of each other's presence. The groups had their own cabins, and though they shared a mess hall, swimming area, recreation room, and athletic field, their movements through the campground were carefully orchestrated so they would not cross paths. That is, until one day when one of the groups, the Rattlers, overheard the other group, the Eagles, playing on the athletic field as they walked through the woods nearby. After the groups became aware of each other, they expressed an interest in playing each other in a game of baseball. The researchers, to create competition over scarce resources, planned a tournament of various games and contests with prizes for the winning group. During the period of competition, the groups began name-calling, teasing, making up derogatory songs, and raiding each other's cabins. After a while, the groups couldn't stand each other.

At that point, the researchers began their strategy for reducing the friction between the groups. The competitions were ended and contact between the groups was arranged for various tasks. However, mere contact was not enough to reduce the friction. The researchers introduced a number of superordinate goals, such as moving large boulders to "fix a problem" with the camp's water system, pooling the groups' money to pay for a film both groups wanted to see, pulling a stalled truck with a rope, and so on. After engaging in these activities and achieving several of their superordinate goals, the groups were civil, even friendly, with each other.[59]

What else can organizations do to minimize intergroup conflict?

· **Create a superordinate category.** A superordinate category is a larger category that subsumes the smaller social groups in the organization. Creating a culture in which employees perceive different groups as part of an organization-wide group or team with everyone sharing common goals can reduce intergroup conflict.
· **Flatten organizational structures in order to reduce status differences.** Although flatter hierarchies can lead to less formal communication and perhaps incivility, the tensions that naturally occur as a result of clearly delineated groups and status differences will be curtailed.
· **Decrease the competition over scarce resources.** Make sure that groups have the resources they need. Scarce resources should be distributed in ways that de-emphasize competition between groups.
· **Use "we" statements.** Using "we" statements instead of "I" statements, and "us" statements instead of "me" statements, communicates a larger, single category.

INTRAGROUP FACTORS

The complete absence of all conflict within a group is not a desirable state. The tendency for people in a group to always agree, conform to the group, and avoid openly dissenting (even though they may be dissenting privately) is sometimes called "groupthink" and can lead to tragic outcomes. After the space shuttle *Challenger* disintegrated before horrified onlookers only moments after its launch, President Reagan appointed a commission to investigate the cause of the accident. The cause was determined to be rocket fuel spewing from a joint that was supposed to be sealed by a failed rubber O-ring. It was also revealed that there had been some concern about the O-rings before the launch. The day before the launch, engineers from the group that manufactured the rocket's motor expressed concerns that the flight might be risky because the O-rings had never been tested below 53 degrees and the morning of the launch was expected to be in the low 20s. They feared the cold would affect the O-rings' resiliency and ability to seal the joint and said the flight should be a "no-go." But NASA launch personnel discounted their concerns and encouraged them to rethink their "no-go" recommendation. After a private meeting with the company's executives, the engineers changed their decision to "A-OK." Jesse Moore, Associate Administrator for Space Flight at NASA Headquarters was at the top of the launch decision chain. He had the power to approve or scrub the shuttle mission. He was advised that the *Challenger* was flight-ready and was told nothing about the concern with the O-rings. He had every reason to believe that everything was "A-OK" at the time of the launch.[60]

Groupthink can happen in highly cohesive groups that discourage dissention within the group and are insulated from other sources of dissenting information. In the *Challenger* example, the engineers were pressured into changing their recommendation and keeping their concerns to themselves. Jesse Moore was shielded by his advisors from the argument for postponing the launch.

Conflict Quote

When we look at the composition of teams within our company, we have found that those with a variety of perspectives are simply the most creative.
—Betsy Holden, Chief Executive Officer, Kraft Foods[61]

Cohesiveness refers to the feelings of attraction the members of the group have for the group. For members of highly cohesive groups, membership is desirable and important. High cohesion does not automatically mean that a group will suffer from the disastrous decision making associated with groupthink. That sort of problem occurs when maintaining the chummy atmosphere of the group takes priority over making good decisions. In general, group cohesion is desirable and is positively related to levels of cognitive conflict and, as might be expected, negatively related to affective conflict.[62]

Groups develop their own implicit and explicit rules and expectations for behavior. Patterns of communication develop that define relationships within the group. Some members of the group will be closer to each other than other members and will form coalitions. Those who are coalesced will communicate with each other more, share more information, and feel closer to each other. Coalitions tend to form for a reason. Those who are closer may have more in common or give each other support. More than one coalition may form, but not everyone in the group will necessarily be included in any coalitions. Isolates, or those excluded from the coalition, may feel left out and rationalize their exclusion by asserting their disinterest in becoming part of a coalition. Among those who are in the coalition, an ingroup bias can develop, with the rest of the group viewed as an outgroup.[63]

Managers can analyze the relationships within a group by looking at the behaviors and patterns of communication among the group members. Particularly important in conflict situations are patterns of behavior that are repeated and lead to the same undesirable outcome. As with interpersonal relationships, toxic patterns of interaction occasionally develop in groups; however, group members may be too tightly connected as a system to recognize the problem and correct it themselves. Managers can learn about these patterns by observing the behavior of group members and, more directly, through interviews. Interview questions can guide group members to explore the spoken and unspoken rules of the group that may be contributing to conflicts.

Questions such as "Whose rule is this?" or "What purpose does this rule serve and what would happen if it were broken?" can help the group members recognize unspoken rules, consider if a rule makes sense, and think about how it relates to their conflict.[64]

Intragroup conflict has received a great deal of attention from researchers and organizations that are interested in promoting effective teamwork. Teams, as we've all heard, are valued for their ability to develop innovative solutions to problems. The belief behind teams is that more talent at the table will generate more ideas and more wisdom will be available to evaluate them. But the teamwork ideal is about more than just adding together individual talents; rather, it is the synergy of teams that produces outcomes beyond the sum of the individual contributions.

Of course, the desired effect is not always the actual result. Most of us who have worked on teams know that unpleasant team experiences with mediocre outcomes are all too commonplace. Teams are often wrought with conflict that limits their ability to produce. Organizations contribute to this conflict by creating teams with ambiguous goals and no clear purpose. They may also create teams that have more members than are required to do the job. Members in these groups will easily recognize that if they contribute very little to the group, the consequences will be minor. They may feel disconnected from the group because their contribution doesn't seem vital for the group's success. This arrangement can also encourage what is called "social loafing," wherein a member of a group contributes little and allows the rest of the group to carry the weight.[65]

Organizations can help reduce this sort of intragroup conflict by clarifying the purpose and goals of teams and making them no larger than they need to be. In addition, organizations can help lessen team conflict by supporting teams with the resources they need. For example, a virtual team may be more effective if its organization provides the members with equipment for video or web conferencing. In addition, organizations can provide their employees with training on working in teams. Research has shown that having even one trained member on a team significantly improves outcomes. For groups, process determines outcome, and if groups have no tools in the form of techniques for managing meetings, the group is likely to spend time deciding and redeciding how things should be done, leading to frustration and conflict. Training can provide the team with these valuable tools.

IDENTIFYING FACTORS IN EMPLOYEE CONFLICTS

Managers can spend a great deal of their valuable time addressing employee conflicts or dealing with their fallout. But it is a mistake for managers to become involved in *all* employee conflicts. Before taking any action, managers must determine if the conflict is constructive or destructive. *Constructive conflict* is desirable, and though it may warrant monitoring to ensure that it doesn't spiral into a *destructive conflict,* it should probably be left alone. For managers dealing with destructive conflicts among employees, one of the important judgments they will need to make is determining whether there is a business problem associated with the conflict and, if so, what it is. Identifying the business problem can help a manager gauge the need for intervention, prioritize the issues, and evaluate potential strategies for resolving the conflict. Managers must also identify the important parties (or *stakeholders*) in the conflict, the level of interdependence between them, and any situational or structural factors that may be contributing to the conflict. It can be helpful to use a guide such as the one in Table 2-4.

It is possible that through this process a manager may think of a solution to the problem that does not involve bringing the parties together to meet. For example, two departments that share a resource may produce a need that exceeds the resource's capacity, creating conflict. If more of the resource is made available, then the conflict is solved. This sort of solution could potentially be produced without even interviewing the parties individually.

An interview with the conflicting parties will be essential for solving more complex issues or serious conflicts. It's also necessary when simply solving the business problem isn't enough because the conflict has become destructive and will continue, even when the substantive aspects of the conflict are solved. Managers may interview the parties separately to get a sense of the history of the conflict from each party's perspective. While a number of factors that may contribute to the conflict may not be explicitly stated in an interview, the way parties talk about a conflict can often reveal them. By talking to those involved, managers may discern the type of conflict, the parties' goals, the conflict management styles of the parties, and what outcomes would satisfy everyone involved.[66]

Table 2-4   Guide for Analyzing Employee Conflicts

Factors in the Conflict:	Questions to Ask:	Response Strategy Notes:
Level of Conflict:	Who are the parties? What levels of conflict are involved? Are special considerations necessary, given the level of conflict? If so, have these been addressed?	
Personality and Style of the Parties:	What is known about the personalities of the parties that could contribute to the conflict? What conflict management	

	styles have the parties demonstrated so far? Is the style appropriate for the type of conflict and other circumstances?	
Relationship of the Parties:	What is the relationship between the parties? What is the nature of their interdependence? How is power distributed between the parties? How much trust exists between the parties?	
Structural Factors:	What are the primary stressor in the work environments of the parties? Are there policies, procedures, or norms contributing to the conflict?	
Messages/Feedback	Is verbally aggressive language being used? Are ineffective communication tactics being used? Is the communication climate defensive? What is being communicated nonverbally?	

In addition to helping the manager better understand the conflict, an interview can help all parties think about their conflict and clarify the issues. In organizations, people can be at odds over any number of issues. Managers can help them determine which issues are most significant and help them focus on a limited number of issues at one time. Importantly from the manager's perspective, interviews can help focus the attention of the parties on the business problem that must be solved.

The most important thing for a manager to do during the interview is to listen. Questions should be open-ended and nondirective. An interview is an information-gathering session. It may be that the manager is able to recognize a solution to conflict during the interview, but that's not really the goal.

Here are some sample open-ended, nondirective questions for interviewing:

- So, tell me what's going on.
- Can you tell me how you got to this point?
- What happened next?
- How would you describe this relationship?
- What would you like to see happen here?
- Who has been involved in this situation to this point?
- Who do you think needs to be brought in on this?
- How do you think this person feels about this situation?

Other useful techniques can be employed to help people identify which issues are the most important. For conflict between groups, a simple procedure is to have the group members write down their ideas about the most important issues. The ideas are then collected and recorded on a flip chart without any information identifying the contributor of the idea. Then, all members at the meeting have a chance to discuss the ideas and seek clarification on the meaning of each idea. After the discussion, the ideas are ranked in order of importance.[67]

Conflict Quote

*At the core, most conflict is about needs that
have not been satisfied—not just physical
needs, but also psychological and
procedural needs. Difficult behavior is often
a result of psychological needs for control,
recognition, affection, and respect.*
—John Ford, Mediation Training Institute[68]

This technique requires that the conflicting groups be in
the presence of each other and communicate about their
ideas. If the two groups are extremely hostile, the *Delphi
Technique* could be used. This approach minimizes face-to-
face communication between the groups during the time that
issues are being identified. The Delphi Technique involves
several steps and is most easily employed if a neutral person
is available to facilitate the process. It begins with all the
people involved writing out answers to open-ended
questions about the issues as they see them. These answers
are collected by the neutral person and read for themes. A
summary of the ideas that emerge are then distributed to all
participants, along with a questionnaire that asks them to
respond to each idea according to some specified criteria.
Those responses are then collected and a summary of the
responses is created and distributed. Persons are asked if
they would like to revise their position on the issues in light
of this new information or if they would like to justify their
position. These responses are collected and again a summary
of them is created and distributed. The participants then give
their final ranking. The process takes the parties from a
general to specific definition of the most important issues
without requiring them to be in the same room before the
issue is well defined.[69]

At this point, managers will have a clear enough
understanding of their employees' conflict to determine
whether collaborative communication between the parties is
the best path to a solution. Managers must also determine if
they themselves can guide the parties to a resolution or if the

help of a professional third party, such as a mediator, is needed. These options will be discussed in Chapter 3.

ANALYZING YOUR OWN CONFLICTS

In some ways, analyzing our own conflicts can be more difficult than analyzing employee conflicts. The main complication is our subjectivity. We know our side of the story. We see the situation from our perspective. In addition, we are more likely to be emotionally involved in our own conflicts, making it even more difficult to analyze them objectively. Because we interpret events through the biases of our own perceptions, understanding our tendencies and predispositions can only help us better understand our conflicts. True understanding of our own personal conflicts requires a true understanding of ourselves. Sometimes we find ourselves upset by something or in conflict with someone, and we don't really understand why. Occasionally, we may find that a conflict has more to do with something about ourselves than the behavior of the other party.

So how do we get to know ourselves better? In his book, *Listening to Conflict,* Erik Van Slyke talks about interpersonal zones for people to explore when learning about themselves. He recommends paying particular attention to our *comfort zones* and *hot zones.* Most of us are familiar with the term **comfort zone** and know this refers to being in a situation where we are comfortable, at ease, and confident. A **hot zone** is outside our comfort zone, where we experience anxiety or strong negative emotions. Research shows that when we have strong emotions, we will look around our environment to find reasons for them. That means that sometimes simply being outside our comfort zone can contribute to conflict. Inside a hot zone, you may feel stressed, mentally exhausted, frustrated, or even helpless. Knowing what triggers these emotions in you can help you when you analyze your own conflicts. Many times, underlying a conflict is a hot zone.[70]

Other interpersonal zones that Van Slyke recommends exploring include *values zones, social zones,* and *cognitive zones.* **Values zones** are created by our beliefs about what is important and what is right or wrong. Knowing what we value and how to prioritize our values can help us to avoid frustration, ineffectiveness in life, and mistakes, as well as help us to understand and possibly avoid certain conflicts. In organizations, groups or individuals in conflict inevitably have different values at the top of their values priority lists. For example, research and development may value speed and innovation, while accounting may value detail and routine. Knowing how we prioritize our values is important, and living in a way that reflects that prioritization can improve the overall quality of our lives and help us to avoid a great deal of intrapersonal and interpersonal conflict.[71]

Social zones refer to our preferences and tendencies regarding social interaction. People vary in interpersonal needs such as the need for affection, the need to be included in social groups, and the need to control others. One common distinction among social interaction preferences is extroversion versus introversion. Extroverts thrive on interactions with others, while introverts are drained by them.

Cognitive zones refer to our preferred strategies for dealing with information. Some people prefer facts, details, logic, and pragmatism and use an analytic strategy for evaluating information. On the other hand, some people prefer principles, summaries, instincts, and flexibility and use an empathic strategy for evaluating information that is people-oriented and subjective.
4

Knowing about our interpersonal zones can help us recognize when we are reacting to one of our zones rather than the actual behavior of another person.[72] Imagine an introvert and an extrovert working together on a project. One needs to be alone to think, the other has to be talking to someone to develop ideas. The extrovert may have a high need for inclusion and control, while the introvert may want to limit the relationship to the project only and to have more independence. This combination could make for a great deal of conflict, but much of it would be about different interpersonal preferences rather than about issues. In a situation of this sort, time might be spent trying to solve conflicts by changing the other person. If the introvert and extrovert understood their own preferences better, they would be less likely to interpret different choices as a source of conflict.

Conflict Quote

The trick is to reframe the situation in your mind and to focus on the things that you can control.

—Paul Stoltz, Organizational Consultant[73]

To analyze any particular conflict, we might begin by considering the conflict history. A major difficulty with considering what happened is that we only have one side of the story. We know our perceptions of the events surrounding the conflict, but we don't know the perceptions of the other party. When we analyze the history of the conflict, we can begin to balance our view by asking ourselves a few questions.

- **What was our contribution to this conflict?** Typically, when we think about our conflicts, we blame others for their part. But few conflicts are the result of only one party's actions. Considering our contribution to the problem, as well as that of the other party, increases our power to change the outcomes in the future.[74]
- **Are we trying to interpret events using beliefs that don't really work for us?** We all have belief systems, which we use to interpret our world. These may include beliefs that we have held for a very long time, perhaps since childhood, and validity of those beliefs may never have been examined. If we examine our beliefs, we may find some beliefs that contribute to our conflict are

without foundation and which could, perhaps, be changed. A manager, for example, may hold the belief that *working mothers are unreliable employees.* This belief may affect the manager's decisions about assignments and promotions. Perhaps this belief is based on a previous experience with a working mother, but a generalization to all working mothers is not really warranted. The manager may examine the belief and determine that it needs to be updated or revised.

- **Are we making any unjustified inferences?** Perhaps we are making negative inferences about another party when they're not really warranted. For instance, "The quality of her work is poor" is an observation about behavior, but "She doesn't care about her job" is an inference that frames the behavior in a negative way. Alternatively, "There is something interfering with her performance" allows for many possible reasons for the behavior. During a conflict, an unjustified inference we frequently make is confusing impact with intention. Someone does something that has a negative impact on us and we conclude that the person's intent was to do us harm. But, very often, harming us was not the intention of the other party. That may not make the act any less harmful, but it does make it more likely that we can work through our conflict with that other person.[75]

- **What does the other person think happened?** We already know our perceptions, and trying to imagine the other person's perceptions can help us understand the conflict better and help us understand our own contributions. When we are involved in conflict, we think we are right and the other person is wrong. We must remember that the other person may very well feel the same way about us.[76]

While sorting through a conflict, we must also address our feelings. It is tempting to avoid the feelings issue, especially in a work context, but conflicts are by their very nature emotional events, some to a higher degree than others. Feelings can be at the very core of a conflict, and if we attempt to ignore them, our feelings may well leak out slowly or in an uncontrollable outburst. Furthermore, we are in poor condition to work through a conflict with the other

97

person if our own feelings are hurt. Hurt feelings can interfere with our ability to listen well and certainly diminish our motivation to take the other person's view.[77]

Our feelings are often tied to identity issues we may experience during conflicts. When we are engaged in conflict, we may question what the conflict means to us in terms of how we see ourselves and how others see us. Conflicts can affect our feelings of competence and self-worth. These issues are often not openly expressed during a conflict and are frequently buried under more explicit concerns in the conflict. We may have to dig a little to understand them, but because conflicts that threaten our identities can feel very serious and send us into an emotional tailspin, understanding these issues can be important and beneficial.[78]

Understanding our conflicts also requires considering our goals and their related issues. Issues can be objective, as with content goals or process goals; or they can be personal, as with identity goals and relational goals. Objective issues tend to have less emotional arousal attached, but, if mishandled, these issues can quickly become personal. Personal issues usually involve more intense emotion. When conflicts involve personal issues and intense feelings, our goals may not be the ones we appear to be arguing about. We may, in fact, argue over a content goal when an identity goal or relational goal is the real source of trouble.[79]

Using a guide like the one offered for analyzing employee conflicts in Table 2-4 may be useful for ensuring that you consider those contributing factors in your analysis. However, your analysis of your own conflict can be more complete, since you have information about your perceptions and feelings that you wouldn't necessarily have about an employee. The guide in Table 2-5 may be a useful tool for analyzing your own conflicts.

As you begin to analyze *your* conflict, you will need to decide whether or not to raise the issue with the other party. By completely analyzing the conflict before raising the issue, you have an opportunity to prepare yourself to do so effectively. You also have the opportunity to determine if there is a better way to solve the problem. You may determine that the conflict is really the result of differences in interpersonal needs or unexamined beliefs. You may determine that the conflict is really more about your reaction to the other party rather than the behavior of the other party.

If you determine that an issue must be raised with someone else, you will benefit from possessing the communication tools needed to work through conflict collaboratively. Whether it is your conflict or the conflict of your employees, resolving it in a way that satisfies all parties and strengthens the relationship between them is only possible through effective communication. In the next chapter, we discuss specific techniques for communicating collaboratively to resolve conflicts.

Table 3-5   Analyzing Your own Conflicts

Questions to Ask Yourself:	Notes:
What do I think happened?	
What does the other person think happened?	
Which of my actions contributed to this conflict? (If you answer "none" to this question, begin reading this book over again.)	
What goals do I have at stake here? · content · process · relational · identity · values	

Am I ignoring situational factors that may be contributing to this person's behavior? Is it possible there are factors of which I am unaware?	
What are my feelings about this situation? Do my feelings seem appropriate given the goals I've identified? If not, what else is going on?	
What do I need from the other party? What does the other party need from me?	

DISCUSSION QUESTIONS

1. Do most conflicts occur at more than one level? Think of examples to support your answer.

2. One of the contributors to workplace conflict is the stress of having too much to do in too little time. In tight economic times, organizations may not be able to hire more workers to relieve the workload. What else can they do to relieve the stress the employees feel?

3. Discuss your current or previous place of employment in terms of the factors that contribute to conflict. What about the organization contributed to conflict and what about it helped prevent conflict?

4. Why do employees of low power express their conflicts indirectly? What is the danger of this type of expression for the organization? What can managers do to encourage a more constructive means of dealing with conflict?

5. If you are in a conflict, is it possible to influence the conflict management style that the other party is using? How could you do so?

6. Is it easier to analyze your own conflicts or the conflicts of your employees? Explain your answer.

7. Under what circumstances would you consider it best not to raise an issue with another party? Would you ever suggest to an employee that he or she not raise an issue? When and why? What impact, if any, would you expect that advice to have on the employee's feelings about you and the organization?

ENDNOTES

1. Douglas Stone, Bruce Patton, and Sheila Heen, *Difficult Conversations* (New York: Viking, 1999).
2. William Wilmot and Joyce Hocker, *Interpersonal Conflict,* 6th ed. (New York: McGraw-Hill Higher Education, 2001).
3. Kristin Bihary, Eaton Corporation, telephone interview, Cleveland, OH, February 26, 2003.
4. Hutchinson, S., telephone interview, December 18, 2002. Integra Realty Resources, Inc., New York, NY. The random telephone survey of 1,206 working adults in the continental U.S. has a margin of error of plus or minus 3%, and was conducted with the assistance of Opinion Research Corporation International of Princeton, N.J. The study was conducted November 8 to November 12, 2001.
5. Jennifer Daw, "Road Rage, Air Rage, and Now 'Desk Rage,'" *Monitor on Psychology,* July/August (2001): 53.
6. Carol Hymowitz and Rachel Emma Silverman, "Can Workplace Stress Get Worse?" *The Wall Street Journal,* January 16, 2001, B1, Column 2 and B4, Column 3.
7. Integra Realty Resources.
8. Jennifer Wirth, "Ban Office Romance, Many Say," *The Cincinnati Enquirer,* November 25, 2002. Online Edition at http://www.enquirer.com.
9. Hymowitz and Silverman.
10. Gary W. Evans, "Behavioral and Physiological Consequences of Crowding in Humans," *Journal of Applied Social Psychology,* 9 (1979): 27–46.
11. Nissen, Beth. "Overworked, overwrought: 'Desk rage' at work," CNN.com, November 15, 2000.

12. Russell Wild, "Risky Rewards," *Working Woman,* June 2001, 77.
13. Wild.
14. Annie Finnigan, "Different Strokes," *Working Woman,* April 2001, 42–46.
15. John Ford, "Cross Cultural Conflict Resolution in Teams," October 2001. Available: http://www .mediate.com.
16. Ford.
17. Ibid.
18. Wilmot and Hocker.
19. Ibid.
20. Ibid.
21. Ibid.
22. Rahim.
23. Wilmot and Hocker.
24. Ibid.
25. Ibid.
26. Rahim.
27. Wilmot and Hocker.
28. Rahim.
29. Lourdes Munduate, Juan Ganaza, José Peiro, and Martin Euwema, "Patterns of Styles in Conflict Management and Effectiveness," *The International Journal of Conflict Management,* 10 (1999): 5–24.
30. Rahim.
31. Wilmot and Hocker.
32. Ibid.
33. Dean Keith Simonton, "Personality and Politics," in *Handbook of Personality Theory and Research,* edited by Lawrence A. Pervin (New York: Guilford Press, 1990), 670–692.
34. Paul Falcone, "When Employees Have a 'Tude," *HR Magazine,* 46 (June 2001): 189–194.
35. J. R. P. French and B. H. Raven, "The Bases of Personal Power," in *Group Dynamics,* edited by J. D. Cartwright and A. Zander (Evanston, IL: Row, Peterson, 1962), 607–622.
36. Wilmot and Hocker.
37. Ibid.
38. Ibid.
39. Willem F. G. Mastenbroek, *Conflict Management and Organization Development* (Chichester, England: Wiley, 1993).

40. John Ford, "Dealing with Difficult Behavior," December 2001. Available: http://www .mediate.com.
41. Mastenbroek.
42. Ibid.
43. Steven A. Beebe, Susan J. Beebe, and Mark V. Redmond, *Interpersonal Communication: Relating to Others* (Boston: Allyn and Bacon, 1999).
44. Daniel Goleman, *Working with Emotional Intelligence* (New York: Bantam Books, 1998).
45. Erik J. Van Slyke, *Listening to Conflict: Finding Constructive Solutions to Workplace Disputes* (New York: Amacom, 1999).
46. Susan Fritz, William F. Brown, Joyce P. Lunde, and Elizabeth Banset, *Interpersonal Skills for Leadership* (Upper Saddle River, NJ: Prentice Hall, 1999).
47. Wilmot and Hocker.
48. Sharon S. Brehm, *Intimate Relationships,* 2nd. ed. (New York: McGraw-Hill, 1992).
49. A. Mehrabian, *Nonverbal Communication* (Chicago: Aldine-Atherton, 1972).
50. J. Larry Goff and Roy A. Cook, "Coming of Age with Self-Managed Teams: Dealing with a Problem Employee," *Journal of Business and Psychology,* 16 (2002): 485–496.
51. Alex Thio, *Sociology* (New York: Longman, 1998).
52. Thio.
53. Rahim.
54. Linda L. Putnam, "Communication and Interpersonal Conflict in Organizations," *Management Communication Quarterly,* 1 (1988): 293–301.
55. Wilmot and Hocker.
56. Michael Billig and Henri Tajfel, "Social Categorization and Similarity in Intergroup Behavior," *European Journal of Social Psychology,* 3 (1973): 27–52.
57. Melanie L. Harrington, "Diversity or Diversion?" *Black Enterprise,* 32, issue 12 (July 2002).
58. Rahim.
59. Muzafer Sherif, O. J. Harvey, B. Jack White, William R. Hood, and Carolyn W. Sherif, *The Robbers Cave Experiment: Intergroup Conflict and Cooperation* (Middletown, CT: Wesleyan University Press, 1988).
60. Diane Vaughan, *The Challenger Launch Decision* (Chicago: University of Chicago Press, 1996).
61. Finnigan.

62. Ensley, Pearson, and Amason.
63. Wilmot and Hocker.
64. Ibid.
65. Bibb Latane, Kipling Williams, and Stephen Harkins, "Many Hands Make Light the Work: The Causes and Consequences of Social Loafing," *Journal of Personality and Social Psychology,* 37 (1979): 822–832.
66. Daniel Dana, *Conflict Resolution* (New York: McGraw-Hill, 2001).
67. Wilmot and Hocker.
68. Ford, "Dealing with Difficult Behavior."
69. Myra Warren Isenhart and Michael Spangle, *Collaborative Approaches to Resolving Conflict* (Thousand Oaks, CA: Sage, 2000).
70. Van Slyke.
71. Ibid.
72. Ibid.
73. Cheryl Dahle, "Don't Get Mad—Get over It!" *Fast Company,* vol. 22, February 1999, http://www.fastcompany.com/online/22/toolbox.html.
74. Van Slyke.
75. Stone, Patton, and Heen.
76. Ibid.
77. Ibid.
78. Ibid.
79. Wilmot and Hocker.

CHAPTER

3

WORKING THROUGH CONFLICT

What is the best way to work through a conflict? Your analysis of the contributing factors based on the communication systems approach in Chapter 2 will help you make that determination. An analysis of the conflict will help you determine if there are easy changes you can make to the context (e.g., increase resources, change procedures) to solve the conflict, or if collaborative communication will be the best choice. Whether you are facing confronting another person in one of your own conflicts or thinking about acting as a mediator for a conflict between your employees, there are some important considerations before deciding to use communication to work through a conflict. What factors should you consider when making the decision to use collaborative communication versus some other means of dealing with the conflict?

∞ Could practical structural changes be made that will end or improve this conflict? If so, consider if these changes will be easier than a difficult conversation between parties. Consider if the real issue might be the structural factors and the impact they are having on the conflict system. Perhaps communicating won't actually do any good if the structural or contextual issues are not addressed. Changes to the context of the conflict system can sometimes be the easiest way to have a lasting impact. Jake owned a small Italian restaurant and thought it would be a great idea to have an ongoing wine selling competition between the members of his small wait staff. Every week, the server who sold the most wine would win a prize. The unforeseen consequence of this idea was the end of the cooperative spirit his wait staff used to share. Servers became less likely to help each other, which led to negative attitudes, bad feelings, backstabbing and lots of conflict. The simple solution for Jake was to end the contest. If you have not identified factors in the context contributing to the conflict, you may have no other choice but to use communication.

∞ Are the parties involved capable communicating in a way that will allow for constructive management of the conflict? Some people simply lack the communication tools needed for collaborative communication. You can't expect people to do something they simply don't have the resources for. Furthermore, you can't expect people to perform well in a situation where they are significantly disadvantaged. If one party is able to communicate exceedingly well, and the other party lacks good communication skills, a power differential exists that can negatively affect the process and lead to parties feeling more frustrated with each other.

∞ Are the parties too hostile to communicate effectively? Sometimes parties experience too much anger to sit down with each other and communicate civilly. Don't try to force parties to do something they seem emotionally unable to do. If you are a party in a conflict and your emotions are beyond your control, wait until you are better able to manage your emotions to communicate with the other party. If you are trying to facilitate or mediate this meeting, you need to be confident in your ability to handle the situation if the conversation gets heated and emotions get fired up. What will you do if the parties start yelling at each other and pointing fingers? If you expect this to happen, you might want to try something other than collaborative communication.

∞ A final question is about trust. Do the parties trust each other? Parties must have some trust in each other to use collaborative communication. They must be willing to share information about themselves in order for other people in the conflict to understand their needs and wants. Without trust, this openness is unlikely. Trust can be increased during the process of collaborative communication, so a lack of initial trust is not an immediate deal breaker. Another valid question is: *Should* parties trust each other? It is perhaps the less common situation, but certainly there are times when one party actually is out to get the other party and collaborative communication is ill-advised because any information shared may be used against the person in the future. If you are in a conflict with a party that you can't trust, you need to protect yourself. This necessary cautiousness; however, will impede the collaborative communication process and you should be aware that the process will be affected if you don't feel you can communicate honestly and openly. If you are helping your employees and you know one of the employees can't be trusted, don't push them into this process. It can end badly.

In this chapter, we will begin by reviewing techniques for working through your own conflicts and helping your employees work through theirs once the decision has been made to raise a conflict issue and address using collaborative communication. We'll look at using dialogue to build relationships while working through conflicts. And we'll describe communication tools that can be used to accomplish this objective, specifically, the collaborative mindset, effective listening and feedback, and positive language (see Table 3-1). We will then explore how managers can act as mediators to help employees work through their conflicts and examine options for bringing in a professional third party when manager-mediation is inappropriate or when a conflict is more than a manager can handle.

RAISING AN ISSUE

Once you've decided that collaborative communication is the way to go, you have one other important decision to make: Are you really going to do it? Remember the fear we discussed in Chapter 1? Here is where you might experience it. People are generally a bit uneasy about raising an issue with another party. Sometimes this unease will lead us to avoid confronting the other party, and instead just dealing with whatever is frustrating us, at least until whatever that is becomes more uncomfortable than the thought of confronting the other party.

But here's something to remember that might tip the scales toward raising the issue with the other party. Moving out of avoidance by raising an issue allows people to share important information about each other and the situation they find themselves in, including complaints that others may be completely unaware of. Raising an issue allows people to communicate about the importance of their relationship and attempt to change something they feel should be changed. Only if you raise an issue can you produce a solution with the participation of all parties that ideally will benefit all involved. The bottom line is that conflict managed well through collaborative communication can actually strengthen relationships.[1]

When the objective for raising an issue is resolving a conflict constructively, the very act of doing so can create possibilities for improved relationships by addressing problems rather than letting them quietly escalate. If the point of raising an issue, however, is to convince the other person that she is wrong, to make her feel bad, to admit guilt, or to apologize, you're not quite ready for collaborative communication yet.

Conflict Quote

People don't learn by staring into a mirror; people learn by encountering difference. So, hand-in-hand with the courage to face reality comes the courage to surface and orchestrate conflicts.
—Ronald Heifetz, Director, Leadership
Education Project at Harvard University[2]

Being clear about your goal beforehand is crucial for determining your approach when raising an issue. The experience of Melissa Giovagnoli, a highly sought-after speaker and trainer, provides a case in point. She had agreed to be the keynote speaker for a conference at a subsidiary of optics manufacturer Canon. Just four days before the engagement, the company canceled her speech in an effort to reduce spending. Giovagnoli was understandably upset. "I'll have to eat more than 20 hours of prep time. And I turned down another assignment for this," she thought. At first she considered contacting the company and demanding compensation for the time she had put in. But before she acted, she thought about what that would get her. She would be angry and she would make the company angry. "If I had pointed my finger at them and said, 'You did this to me,' I would have put them on the defensive," says Giovagnoli. Instead, she thought about her long-term goal. If she focused on the immediate content goal, it might be at the expense of any long-term relationship goal. In the end, she called the company and talked to them about how the relationship could be saved. They were able to negotiate a new speaking deal at a lower fee, with some follow-up consulting.[3]

As we have noted, just because parties are capable of collaborative communication that doesn't mean it is the best option for working through a given conflict. This process can be demanding. It can require time, emotional investment, and energy. It's not the best choice for minor issues of negligible consequence and it's probably not the best choice when relationship between the parties is not very important or is just temporary. The collaborative communication process is all about protecting the relationship.

PROTECTING RELATIONSHIPS DURING CONFLICTS

Successful relationships at work, like all other relationships, experience conflict. People who work together will have differences. In successful working relationships, people simply develop ways to deal with them without sacrificing the relationship. Co-workers may resolve some issues and agree to disagree about others, but they are still able to work together well. A successful working relationship means that the parties treat each other with respect and are able to function within the organization, despite their differences.[4]

During conflict, we are often so focused on the substantive issues and the goal of reaching a settlement that we fail to think about the process we use to get there or what that will do to our relationship with the other party. But this is a mistake. In most cases, despite whatever initial reaction we may have to a conflict, we are interested in preserving our connection with the other party. Important relationships in an organizational setting can take a number of forms, many of which have nothing to do with friendship or liking. They can be based exclusively on interdependence, for example. How we go about resolving a conflict in an ongoing association can affect the relationship either positively or negatively. For example, a competing or dominating style that leads to personal attacks, threats, or other coercive techniques can leave relationships damaged, while collaborative problem solving can help a relationship grow. We want, in most cases, to maintain successful working relationships with others in our organization—even those who may be in conflict with us. Thus, the importance of the relationship is a consideration when deciding how to work through the conflict. When a relationship is particularly important to us, we must continually keep in mind the process we use for working through conflict.[5]

When a relationship is far more important than the issue involved, we may choose to become accommodating; however, accommodation isn't a good choice when the issue is important. Ironically, a habit of accommodating can be detrimental to a relationship. Relationships built on one-sided concessions can be fragile, and agreements that are not in the best interest of one can lead to resentment toward the other. Working through conflict constructively, rather than accommodating, can build and strengthen relationships. Constructive conflict resolution encourages people to accept each other as a person of value, even during conflict.[6]

Table 3-1 Communication Tools for Dialogue and Collaborative

Collaborative Mindset	Positive Language	Effective Listening and Feedback
Choosing an attitude of curiosity Separating people from positions Focusing on interests	Reframing Using relational statements Making statements about specific behaviors	Asking questions Listening reflectively Using nonverbal immediacy cues Dealing with emotions

COLLABORATIVE COMMUNICATION AND DIALOGUE

USING DIALOGUE TO ACHIEVE COMMUNICATION OBJECTIVES

Working through conflict constructively is the result of effective communication. Plainly put, the communication we use in the conflict resolution process will determine the content and relational outcomes that we achieve. During conflict, we can speak about winning, fighting for our rights, getting what we deserve, or being in the right. We can also talk about blame and fault. We can speak about our options as if they were limited and our position as if it were the only one that would do. All of which will create a competitive win/lose environment and can lead to dissatisfying outcomes and damaged relationships. Alternatively, we can talk about perceptions and contribution, rather than blame. We can talk about creative options, innovative solutions, working together, and collaborative problem solving. All of which create an environment for constructive conflict.[7]

Okay. So you're going to try collaborative communication, but what are you actually going to talk about? What do you need to accomplish through this process to be successful? Whether the conflict is one of your own or one you are helping employees work through, the ultimate goal is to help the parties involved understand each other's perspective and generate solutions that address everyone's interests. To get to that point, you'll need to take a few foundational steps in that direction. You'll need to encourage parties to develop a mindset that will allow them to care about the other person's perspective and be curious enough to learn about it. This is pretty tough if parties think the other person has intentionally harmed them. Curiosity isn't usually our first reaction when we think someone has wronged us, so parties have to get past blaming and faultfinding.

You'll also need to get parties to the point where they are willing to share their perspective. If parties don't trust each other or don't trust the process, this will be tough. If you manage the process well, trust can be increased. This effectiveness of process also depends largely on good listening. Parties must listen to each other in a way that encourages disclosure. In other words, in a way that is nonjudgmental and makes the other party feel heard. In this chapter you will be given communication tools helpful for establishing trust, encouraging effective listening, and for managing the collaborative communication process and fostering dialogue.

Dialogue, as we use the term here, refers to communication between parties that emphasizes learning about each other's perspective. The goal is sharing information and creating common meaning through communication, as opposed to arguing or persuading which is often the goal of conflict communication. Using dialogue can help us overcome communication barriers and accomplish our communication goals better understanding and an improved relationship. Dialogue is more than a conversation between two people. It is an approach to communication characterized by acceptance, genuineness, and an effort to fully understand and empathize with the other person.[8] While poor communication can damage relationships, dialogue is a form of communication that respects relationships. It honors individuals and differences in perspective. Through dialogue, people attempt to get to know each other's perspectives and look at things from another frame of reference. It makes it possible for each to explore differences and commonalities. It also allows the meaning that is being constructed through the communication of each person to come to light.[9]

The goal of dialogue is the shared construction of meaning that occurs during the communication process. But a common meaning of a message is by no means a guaranteed outcome of the process. Each participant— senders, receivers, and observers—brings his or her own special filters (sometimes called "lenses") to the process, distorting or shaping how the message and its content are received and interpreted. *Perception is the process of selecting, organizing, interpreting, and assigning meaning to the information that we receive through our senses.*[10] How we perceive or interpret stimuli in our immediate environment depends on a number of factors, including culture, personality, experience, and mood. Therefore, individual perceptions of the same sensory information can vary tremendously. Jurors who hear the same evidence, for example, will often have very different views of what the evidence means in terms of the defendant's guilt or innocence. Thus, *one message sent to two receivers is really two messages.*

Differing perceptions can be at the root of simple misunderstandings. And all communication is complicated by the fact that we each have our own individual approach to interpreting the messages we receive. In some cases, differences in interpretation can lead to serious misunderstandings. These misunderstandings, however, are really pseudo-conflicts and can quickly be cleared up with effective communication that creates a common understanding of meaning.

It is a myth, however, that all conflicts are about misunderstanding. Frequently, people in conflict are very clear about each other's position, and the positions simply oppose one another.[11] Yet, even in these cases where there is no misunderstanding of the conflicting parties' messages, differences in perception are still important. Consider the story of two project managers.

Rick was already feeling the stress of a looming deadline for a project that he considered shaky when the day took a turn for the worse. Jack, who had been Rick's partner on the project, told him about a family vacation he had planned for the following month. Jack explained that he would be leaving immediately after the project deadline, which meant, of course, if anything went wrong and the client asked for changes, Jack would be conveniently out of town, and Rick would have to deal with them on his own. Even worse, he might have to deal with the fallout of a missed deadline. When Rick voiced these concerns, Jack responded with a glib indication of his confidence that Rick "could handle it." Rick was frustrated with what he perceived to be Jack's lack of responsibility and poor work ethic. He was also upset because he considered Jack a friend, as well as a partner, and expected better treatment from him. By the end of the day, Rick let Jack know exactly how he felt in a way that only made things worse.

The conflict that Rick is experiencing with Jack revolves around differences in their perceptions of the difficulty of the project and Jack's vacation plans. Jack may not share Rick's perception of the project being "shaky" and may think that Rick's concern about last-minute problems and missing the deadline are baseless. Rick, on the other hand, sees Jack's vacation plans as irresponsible and inconsiderate, but Jack most likely doesn't share that perception. Interestingly enough, both managers probably have the same ultimate goal of completing the proposal on time and doing good work, but they differ in how they want to go about achieving that goal. Furthermore, their definitions of "good work" may not be the same.

Our perceptions will influence our communication, and the way we communicate during a conflict helps shape our perceptions. The way we talk about conflict and the messages we create when we are in conflict will determine the experience we have, as well as the outcomes that are possible. A study performed by Elizabeth Loftus, the psychologist well known for her work on eyewitness testimony, illustrates the profound effect that changing just one word in a message can have on how an event is interpreted and remembered. In her study, participants were shown a film of a car accident in which two cars collide. They were then asked questions about what they saw. Some participants were asked how fast the cars were going when they "smashed" into each other, while others were asked how fast the cars were going when they "hit" each other.

115

Those participants asked the "smashed" question gave significantly higher estimates of speed than those who were asked the "hit" question. Not only did the two groups' interpretation of the event differ in terms of estimated speed, but their memory of the event was affected by the word change, as well. A week after viewing the film, the participants were contacted again and asked if they remembered seeing broken glass at the accident. There was no broken glass in the film, but those who were asked the "smashed" question were more than twice as likely as those who were asked the "hit" question to remember seeing broken glass.[12]

When the perceptions of the messages sent during conflict communication are true to the meanings of the messages, there can still be misperception about what lies behind the messages. In other words, the message could be understood, but the motives, intentions, or logic behind the message could be misperceived. An employee, for example, could perceive a directive from her boss as being restrictive and controlling, while the boss may perceive the directive to be considerate and helpful. This type of misperception can lead to conflicts in which people argue over conclusions based on misperceptions ("You are trying to control me") rather than the behavior that led to the conclusion ("I felt controlled when you gave me that direction"). Often our conclusions contain inferences about other people's intentions. Arguing over conclusions is rarely effective in reaching a solution to conflict for several reasons.[13]

- When we argue our conclusions, the other party has no way of knowing how we arrived at them.
- Arguing our conclusions implies that we have enough information to come to a correct conclusion, but we may not have all the information.
- And, even if we have the same basic information as the other party, arguing our conclusions usually ignores the other party's perspective or interpretation of the information.

People engaged in conflict often become grounded in their own perception, unable or unwilling to take another's perspective. We can have a difficult time widening our span of tolerance to include perceptions that are quite different from our own. This difficulty is in part because, according to our life experience, our perception is correct. It's easy to forget that the other person in a conflict feels the same way about his or her perspective.

Constructive conflict resolution requires learning about the perceptions of others. This is not to say that conflicting parties must agree with the other's perspective, but rather they must demonstrate a willingness and desire to discover what it is. Differing perceptions can play an important role in the initiation and maintenance of conflict, but understanding and tolerating varying perceptions can create opportunities for conflict management and resolution. When conflicting parties begin to understand each other's real interests, this perception may change. And by exploring each other's perspectives and learning what really matters, conflicting parties are often able to generate innovative solutions that allow both parties to satisfy their interests.[14]

The process requires two things: The right attitude and the right technique. Next we'll discuss the collaborative mindset, or the attitude needed to engage in dialogue. Then we'll introduce communication tools to help you effectively manage the process.

THE COLLABORATIVE MINDSET

DEVELOP AN ATTITUDE OF CURIOSITY

When a conflict is complex, you improve your chances of achieving your goal when raising an issue if you prepare by analyzing the conflict and considering the contributing factors, as we suggested in Chapter 2. Content or substantive issues tend to be the most obvious but may be only a minor part of the conflict. Process, relational, identity, or values issues may be involved as well. (The involvement of these issues is especially likely when the relationship between the parties is important.) You can manage yourself better—particularly your emotions—during interactions with the other person if you do some advance thinking about the true nature of the conflict, your own feelings, and the probable feelings of the other person.

The dialogue process contributes to successful outcomes in conflict resolution because it enables people to understand each other better. Conflicts are about perceptions, and understanding perceptions is vital to working through them successfully. By comparison, objective reality may be of little help in resolving our differences. Imagine, for example, that you meet with a new prospect. He calls to reject your pitch on a day when you aren't available. He insists on speaking to someone that day and the co-worker who takes his call talks him into a deal. You and your co-worker may agree on the objective reality of these events and still not agree on how the commission should be split. To work through such conflicts we have to develop an attitude of true curiosity about the other person's perspective.[15]

Only with clear understanding of each other's perceptions and concerns can people in conflict work collaboratively to produce a satisfying solution. When we initially analyze a conflict, we think about the problem and try to understand the contributing factors. But at that point, we still have just one side of the story: our own. The true nature of the conflict and possible solutions may not emerge until we communicate openly with the other party. Effective communication allows each of us to explore the other's perspectives and to attempt to create a third perspective that both may share. From this perspective, it is easier for each of us to try to discover what the other person's true interests may be.

But dialogue is neither simple nor easy. It requires a willingness to spend time exploring the other person's point of view. It necessitates a commitment to taking turns listening at a deeper level. It means using language that saves face and asking questions that further the interaction and our own understanding. It's a risky process because it requires us to explore unfamiliar points of view. We may learn that we were wrong or that we did not have all the information we needed when we acted. We may see that, from another person's frame of reference, we contributed greatly to the conflict.[16]

Dialogue also requires an investment of time and energy that we typically wouldn't make unless the relationship were somehow important to us. When we create dialogue, we communicate our acceptance and understanding of other people and our caring for them. This is not the same thing as communicating that we agree with them or that we are accommodating them. Rather, we are simply recognizing their value as people and working to understand them.

Conflict Quote

We generally do not look at conflict as opportunity—we tend to think about conflict as unpleasant, counter-productive and time-consuming. Conflict that occurs in organizations need not be destructive, provided the energy associated with conflict is harnessed and directed towards problem-solving and organizational improvement.
—Robert Bacal, Institute for Conflict Prevention[17]

SEPARATE PEOPLE FROM THEIR POSITIONS

Only if we develop an attitude of true curiosity will we be willing to take the risk and invest the energy required for dialogue. When we really want to know another person's perspective, it shows. But adding to the challenge of dialogue is our tendency to see the other party in the conflict as the problem. Blaming others for conflict does not help solve the problem, even when we feel the blame is justified. Neither does making negative inferences about other people and their motives.

Sometimes we may feel as if the other person views *us* as the problem. We may read something negative into a person's comments, or we may feel as if we are being personally attacked if someone points out an error we've made. We may think another person doesn't like us if he or she opposes our suggestion.[18] And it may be that the other party *does* see us as the problem. Keep in mind that other people's perceptions about how things are in a conflict may vary markedly from our own, and, perhaps, if we viewed the situation from their frame of reference, we would see things just as they do.[19]

Unquestionably, it's hard to engage in dialogue and feel curious about another person's perspective and interests if we think that person really *is* the problem, doesn't like us, or isn't treating us fairly. We need to separate the people from the problem. In other words, we need to focus on troubling behaviors as the problem and not the people or personalities involved. We can work toward separating people issues from the other issues in two ways: First, by recognizing the difference between intentions and impact. And second, by thinking about our conflict as a problem for the relationship that people must solve together, rather than as problems for individuals who must compete to get the best solution for themselves.[20]

Recognizing the difference between impact and intentions can make it much easier for us to think positively about the other party in a conflict. Often, when people do things that hurt us or make us angry, that wasn't really their intention. Recognizing also that the negative consequences we are experiencing are probably unintended can help us to see the problem and the person as separate. Of course, this doesn't make the damage any less significant, but it can help control the damage to the relationship.[21]

FOCUS ON INTERESTS

With traditional conflict resolution approaches, people argue their *positions* rather than their *interests*. A party's interests are their true concerns. For example, two managers may disagree about assigning a particular employee to lead a project team. One manager may be concerned that the employee's department will fall behind in its work if the employee is pulled away for the project. So this manager's interest is the employee's department staying caught up in its work. His position would be to not appoint the employee as team leader. The other manager's interest may be in rewarding the employee for stellar performance with a position of leadership. Her position would be to appoint the employee as team leader.

Any interest may have multiple positions that can satisfy it. However, when people argue their positions, they tend to lock into just one position, usually the most obvious, and argue as if only that position is an acceptable solution to the conflict. In our preceding example, if the managers had stayed focused on their positions, they would have argued back and forth about whether or not to appoint the employee and would never have agreed. Instead, they focused on their interests and found multiple, mutually acceptable solutions to their conflict. They eventually decided to appoint the employee and bring a temporary worker into the department if it were to get behind.

When people argue their positions, their true interests may be hard to recognize. Furthermore, their positions may be about substantive issues, ignoring any relational, identity, or process goals. Engaging in dialogue can help parties communicate openly about interests rather than positions and make possible the production of mutually satisfying solutions through collaborative problem solving.[22]

A CASE IN POINT: WINNING TEAMS LEARN TO MANAGE RELATIONSHIPS

Ernesto Bertarelli, the Swiss biotech billionaire who won the America's Cup—the Holy Grail of international yachting—has never been short of either ambition or ego. He promised to bring the cup back to Europe for the first time since the Americans carried it off in 1851. And he's promised to hoist the trophy atop Switzerland's 13,500-foot Matterhorn as a gesture of defiance to those who said he couldn't win it.

His team *Alinghi's* 5–0 victory in the 2003 sailing match in New Zealand's Hauraki Gulf was the result of more than grand ambition or a large bankroll, however. Much of Bertarelli's success came from his ability to identify and hire the world's best blue water sailors and to manage the egos that come with such skill. Russell Coutts, the skipper who had helped win the cup for New Zealand in 1999, credits Bertarelli's business skill and conflict management abilities for much of their success.

"Ernesto has been absolutely key in the process because he was able to bring a lot of lessons from his business," says Mr. Coutts. "He has a wealth of experience in bringing people together from different countries and cultures and getting them to work effectively."

Mr. Bertarelli may look like a playboy type—he loves sailing big boats, he is married to a former English beauty queen, and he superstitiously calls all his yachts *Alinghi* because it brings him good luck. But he is also a very able manager. He selected his team nearly three years ago and delegated operational management to Mr. Coutts and Michel Bonnefous, a sailing colleague.

By contrast, Larry Ellison, the Oracle chief executive and losing competitor to Bertarelli in the Louis Vuitton Challenge Cup series, hired four of the world's best skippers, interfered in their decision making, and his boat was riven by internal tensions. The last skipper aboard *Oracle,* in fact, sacked Ellison—threw him off the boat.

"In the cup we have a rule that you have to choose your people at the beginning and then cannot change them," says Mr. Bertarelli. "I think that is one of the most important decisions anyone has ever to make, be it in business or in competition—choose your people right."

Source: W. Hall, "Swiss Billionaire Reaches the Pinnacle of Sailing Success," *Financial Times,* Monday, March 3, 2003, 14. See also: W. Hall and G. Dyer, "America's Cup: Playboy Gets Serious," http://www .financialtimes.com, February 26, 2003; http://www .americascup.yahoo.com.

TOOLS FOR THE COMMUNICATION PROCESS

EFFECTIVE LISTENING AND FEEDBACK

Sharing each other's perceptions is only as effective as the listening skills of the parties involved. Effective listening is an integral part of the dialogue process. Dialogue requires **empathic listening** or listening at the deepest level. Empathic listening goes well beyond just hearing what is said. When listening empathically, the listener tries to take the perspective of the speaker.

Conflict Quote

Good listening is fueled by curiosity and empathy: What's really happening here? Can I put myself in someone else's shoes? It's hard to be a great listener if you're not interested in other people.
—Ronald Heifetz, Director, Leadership Education Project at Harvard University[23]

Listening well during a conflict requires a serious effort to overcome the common barriers to effective listening, including removing distractions, paying attention, maintaining eye contact, and not interrupting. But good listening during conflict is even more challenging for several reasons. Emotions may be running high. People may be reluctant to share important information because trust may be low or they may become defensive. Listening

123

empathically is one way to build trust. When people listen to others without becoming defensive or shutting them down, speakers will be more likely to open up and share their perspectives. We can improve our ability to listen during conflicts by using active listening techniques, dealing effectively with emotions, and using appropriate nonverbal communication.

ASKING QUESTIONS

Some people may need encouragement to share their perspectives. Asking them to share their side with us first by using an open-ended question can get things started. If we are nonthreatening and listen well, the person will begin to feel more at ease and speak more freely. We can encourage the flow of information by asking more open-ended, probing questions such as:

· Can you tell me more about that?
· How do you feel about that?
· What did that mean for you?
· How do you see that?

We must be careful when asking questions to further a person's disclosure to avoid phrasing the questions in ways that will put that person on the defensive. Questions that start with "why" or "how could you" often push the respondent into a defensive state. We also want to avoid asking leading questions, or questions that are really statements phrased as a question ("Isn't it true that... ?"). Questions can be phrased in ways that carefully disguise the ego attack contained within them. Obviously, we want to avoid asking questions of this type as well.

Here is a sampling of questions to avoid:

· Why did you do that?
· How could you believe that?
· Don't you think that's right?
· Wouldn't this way be better?
· Surely you can recognize the error, can't you?
· But certainly you must agree with that decision, don't you?

Once a person begins disclosing his or her perspective, we as listeners want to make sure we understand what's being said by asking clarifying questions. Nonjudgmental, clarifying questions allow us to get more information about a point we don't fully understand and check our perceptions of the other person's message for accuracy.

- Can you tell me more about that?
- Could you give me an example of what you mean by that?
- Do you mean... ?
- Is what you're saying... ?

Questions about the future can also be helpful. First, they help us clarify our understanding of what the other party wants as an outcome. Second, they keep us focused on what can be changed rather than finding fault and laying blame for what has already happened. Questions such as, "What can we do differently next time this occurs?" are optimistic and empower each of us to create change.[24]

REFLECTIVE LISTENING

Another way to check our perceptions of another person's message is to use reflective listening. **Reflective listening** is a technique in which the listener reflects, or repeats, back to the speaker the content of the message, the feelings behind the message, and the conclusions of the message. This doesn't mean that the listener parrots exactly what the speaker has said. Rather, the listener is stating in his or her own words what has been communicated.

Consider a situation in which one manager is upset with another for changing the date of a meeting with an important client. The following exchange is, of course, a highly simplified example that lacks the richness and complexity of real life and is meant only to illustrate reflecting content, feelings, and conclusions.

Person 1: You moved that meeting to the 22nd without checking with me. I just got done scheduling an onsite visit with another client for that day, and now I'm going to have to call them back and change those plans. I don't think that makes me—or the company—look very good.

Person 2: Sorry about that. I moved the meeting to a day you already had booked (reflecting content). I don't blame you for being irritated with me (reflecting feeling). I really put you in an awkward position with our other clients, and that could have been avoided if I had checked with you before moving the meeting (reflecting conclusions).

DEALING WITH EMOTIONS

Reflecting feelings while listening is manageable when our emotions are in check, but what happens when they get out of control? Both substantive and relational issues can be laden with emotion—the more important the issues, the more intense the emotions. While some emotions can be useful because they motivate us to do something about a conflict, strong feelings that go unaddressed can make conversation—especially dialogue—difficult. It's hard to see things from another person's perspective if we are consumed with anger or hurt.[25]

Conflict is often associated with feelings of anger and fear. When we feel that we've been wronged or threatened, as we often do during conflict, we will likely feel angry or fearful. We all know that people don't enjoy feeling angry and certainly don't enjoy having anger directed at them. In fact, some parties use extreme emotions to coerce others, knowing that they will give in to escape the unpleasantness of the strong emotions. Anger and fear can be intense and unpleasant emotions, but emotions can be managed. How we respond to our feelings of anger and fear and how we receive others' feelings of anger will determine whether conflict is destructive or constructive.[26]

Very often, feelings are only indirectly expressed during a conflict. They leak into the conversation, not as feelings, but as other things like accusations or judgments. We hear comments such as "You set me up" or "You're inconsiderate" during a conflict. Clearly, emotions lie behind these comments, but nothing about feelings is asserted directly.

Conflict Quote

It can have a profoundly negative effect on those who have to work around the explosive person. It can add to hypertension, stress-related illness.
—Eric Hollander, Professor of Psychiatry[27]

Talking directly about our feelings, saying that we feel angry, hurt, or disappointed, would be a much better way to address those feelings. However, when feelings are mentioned directly, the other person is commonly blamed for them with "you" statements, such as "You make me so angry" or "You hurt my feelings." People on the receiving end of statements like these are likely to respond defensively.

A much more effective way to talk about those feelings is to take responsibility for them, rather than blaming the other person for them, by using "I" statements instead of "you" statements. In other words, we could say something like "I feel disappointed," rather than "You let me down." One of the most effective ways to talk about feelings is to connect them to the specific behaviors of others by making statements such as "When you do *this* in *that* situation, I feel *hurt.*" This approach can allow us to point out the disagreeable behavior without blaming the other person for our feelings.[28]

We also need to be aware that, like us, the other parties in a conflict can have strong feelings. When intense feelings are directed at us, it is even more difficult to manage our own emotions. So how should we respond when other people get angry? We can try to argue them out of it. We can tell them that their feelings are unreasonable or just plain stupid. But that rarely works. We're better off if we acknowledge their feelings. Of course, this is easier said than done because those feelings are likely to be expressed as accusations, judgments, and "you" statements.

Statements like "You are completely unprofessional and totally incompetent" can be difficult to listen to without becoming defensive. The key is to guide the other party away from personal attacks and toward an expression of the feelings behind the attacks. We can do this by reflecting back their feelings: "I know you're very angry right now." Or we could ask them about their feelings directly.

When other people share their feelings with us, we need to acknowledge them, but we don't have to accept responsibility for them. We need to let them know that we hear and understand their feelings, but we do not need to agree that their feelings are our fault. We may want to allow them to vent their feelings because people sometimes feel better after they've had an opportunity to air their grievances and feel like they've been listened to and understood. This is only advisable, however, if we are able to resist responding defensively or attacking them, and they are able to vent without becoming abusive.[29]

Both parties benefit from talking directly about feelings during a conflict without losing control. But as we all know, emotions can be difficult to tame. They may surge unexpectedly, be more intense than we expected, or they may hide and then resurface later. Thinking about our feelings before confronting another person can help us keep our emotions in check.[30] During a conflict, you may experience a number of interwoven feelings. Exploring them in advance of an interaction with someone else can help you understand your full range of feelings and how to handle them during the interaction.[31] Which strategies can you employ for managing your emotions during a confrontation with the other party?

- **Prepare for the emotions you and the other person will experience** before you raise an issue. Think about the feelings they will experience and how those might come out as accusations or judgments. Think ahead about how you will respond to these statements in a way that frames them as feelings about specific behaviors.

· **Detach from the immediate situation.** Sometimes when we are involved in a conflict, it seems to consume us. We can reduce our emotional involvement by reminding ourselves that time will pass. A conflict that seems very important at one point in time can seem like a very minor incident a short time later.

· **Take a time-out.** If you feel yourself losing control, you can take a time-out. You can do this by mentally counting to ten, or you can suggest a cooling down period and simply go for a walk.

· **Stay focused on your goal.** If your communication objective is to resolve a conflict constructively and maintain a good working relationship, you will need to manage your emotions well. Focusing on your goal can help you put your emotions in perspective and prevent you from saying things you will regret.

· **Invite a third party to help.** If emotions are extreme and hostility is intense, you may need to ask a third party to facilitate or mediate any discussion. If you or the other person have become very defensive and can't see past the assignment of blame, you may require a third party to help you communicate.

NONVERBAL IMMEDIACY CUES

Much of our emotion is communicated nonverbally. The tone, pitch, and volume of our voice; our facial expressions; and even our posture communicate how we are feeling. To listen effectively during a conflict, we must use nonverbal cues to communicate our acceptance and caring for the other person.

It can be very difficult, if not downright impossible, to "lie" nonverbally. The problem is having too many things to control. If we focus on maintaining good eye contact and monitoring our facial expression, we might disclose our true feelings through a rigid body posture. Alternatively, if we truly adopt the collaborative mindset, our nonverbal communication will typically bear that out.

POSITIVE LANGUAGE

Positive and negative language both reveal and create our attitudes through the words we use. Negative language focuses on the problem rather than the solution and on limitations rather than possibilities. It has a tone of criticism and blame. Positive language, on the other hand, has an optimistic tone and focuses on what can be done. Reframing is a way of transforming negative language into positive language. Relational statements are optimistic statements about working through conflict and building a relationship. Specific behavioral statements are useful for addressing issues of blame and personal criticism. In the pages that follow, we'll examine each of these forms of positive language in a bit more detail.

REFRAMING

The way we say things, the words we use, create a "frame" that shapes our perceptions. **Reframing is the process of creating a constructive frame or a more positive viewpoint for whatever is going on.** While the objective reality may remain the same, reframing an event can change the meaning entirely. Through the reframing process, we can turn negative or hostile statements into problems to be solved collaboratively. Statements can be reframed in ways that make them more positive, future-oriented, and much more constructive. For example,[32]

- **We can reframe personal attacks:** "You're incompetent" can be changed to "This proposal needs a little more work."
- **We can reframe hostile statements:** "You're rude and thoughtless" becomes "I prefer to be informed of changes in advance."
- **We can reframe statements about the past:** "For the last three weeks you haven't submitted your daily reports on time" could become a statement about the

future, "We could improve operations considerably if these reports were submitted by their deadline."

- **We can reframe criticisms:** "You're unreliable" could become a request, "Could you give me a little advance notice when you won't be able to make the meetings?"

Techniques for reframing include rephrasing, proposing an option, moving from abstract to specific, and moving from positions to interests. Some more creative ways of reframing include creating a metaphor or role-playing.

Conflict Quote

When we reframe, we shift the focus of the argument away from positions and toward identifying the needs and interests that will lead toward resolution. We also might ask for more information that will ensure that we know what this person really means by "trustworthy." Maybe he really means that he cannot "count on our follow-through" or "does not feel supported." These issues differ from "trust." Reframing helps us properly diagnose the problem.
—Erik Van Slyke, *Listening to Conflict*, p. 85[33]

RELATIONAL STATEMENTS

Parties working through conflicts are often anxious. They may have low levels of trust in each other and be concerned that the other party will try to "win the argument." We can create a more relaxed, collaborative atmosphere by making optimistic relational statements such as, "I'm sure we can work this out." In this statement is an implicit invitation for the other party to join us in producing a solution to the conflict. Relational statements communicate that the relationship matters and we are interested in working through the issues *with* the other party to produce a mutually acceptable solution. They reduce the other party's fear that we will attack them personally, react defensively, or try to force a solution on them that is not in their best interest. Relational statements also reduce the likelihood that the other party will attack us.[34] As we work through conflict, periodically making relational statements about what is going well and noting points of agreement can contribute to the collaborative atmosphere.

SPECIFIC BEHAVIORAL STATEMENTS

It is difficult to create change in ourselves, to say nothing of creating change in others, if we're unclear about what exactly should be changed. When problem behaviors are the source of conflict, those specific behaviors should be discussed. Speaking in generalities—or worse, hurling personal criticisms—will do little to create positive change and is likely to escalate a conflict.

When we want others to change we should tell them which specific behavior is a problem for us and what we would like them to do instead. Of course, this doesn't mean they will automatically comply, but at least they'll be clear on what you want from them. Similarly, when others want us to change, if they don't offer a description of our problem behavior, we should ask for one. We can also ask them for some specific examples of what they are talking about. Again, if we hear, "You are completely unprofessional and totally incompetent," it's hard to know where to begin to improve the situation. Alternatively, if we hear, "I think it is unprofessional for you to arrive late to meetings," that's a criticism we can do something about. It helps the understanding of both parties to clarify the specific behaviors involved. This leads away from personal attacks and frames the issue as something that can be addressed.

NEGOTIATION

Negotiation is the process of working through the issues in a conflict. We often think of negotiation as something that is done by politicians, trained FBI agents, top executives, and union leaders. But in reality we all are very experienced negotiators because we do it everyday. When you work out agreements on what time to hold a meeting, or who should staff the booth at a trade show, or even where to go for lunch, you are negotiating. Negotiation is an ongoing part of relationships.

Negotiation is an active phase of conflict resolution that rests somewhere between avoiding a conflict and competing to win. It is a way of moderating conflicts that inhibits destructive behaviors, allows for self-discovery, and encourages trust between parties. During negotiation people mutually attempt to meet their goals by brainstorming ideas, generating many options, and practicing give-and-take. Even though a negotiation may seem to be only about substantive issues, the process of negotiation is really about working through the substantive issues in a way that improves the relationship between the parties.[35]

Negotiation requires that both parties engage in the process, be willing to cooperate, and use persuasive communication rather than manipulation or coercion. Solutions produced through negotiation are often packaged, meaning that a variety of alternatives is generated and the final solution is some combination of these. This works only if the negotiating parties are interdependent and have something to offer each other. Power differences can affect the ability of people to negotiate and trade off options effectively. A low-power party may seek ways to balance power, such as hiring a lawyer.[36]

Despite the potential that negotiation holds, it is often not nearly as effective as it could be. Negotiation frequently turns into positional bargaining. As you read just a few pages back, when people argue about positions instead of interests, they often lock themselves into a position and make it sound as if only one solution would be acceptable. This effect is worsened in negotiation by the fact that people tend to make the first statements of their position more extreme, since they expect to make some concessions. ("I'm willing to pay $200,000, but I'll offer $150,000 to start.") Interests that may be compatible or even shared may not be

133

revealed through arguing positions. In negotiation, arguing over positions is bad for the process and makes satisfying agreement less likely.[37]

Conflict Quote

It's common for negotiators to confuse the deal and the relationship. They feel that if they push too hard to get the best deal possible today, they may jeopardize their company's ability to do business with the other party in the future. Or they fear that if they pay too much attention to the relationship, they'll end up giving away too much and make a lousy deal.

—Danny Ertel, Founding Partner of Vantage Partners LLC[38]

People can have different approaches to the negotiation process, ranging from competitive to collaborative approaches. During the process, people may swing from competitive to collaborative and across all points in between, often beginning with a competitive approach that accomplishes little but soon realizing the advantage of using a collaborative approach.[39]

COMPETITIVE APPROACHES

Competitive approaches are based on the assumption that resources are limited or that the size of the "pie" is fixed and that the only acceptable strategy is a win/lose mindset, where each party tries to get the largest slice of the pie for themselves. Communication patterns of the competitive style include threats, confrontation, and argumentation. Information is often concealed or is misleading. Competitive tactics include opening with high demands and making small and slow concessions that are timed for maximum effect, and then exaggerating their value.[40]

Competitive approaches have several distinct disadvantages. They tend to be shortsighted, based on the assumption that one negotiation will not have an effect on later relations, but, of course, it can. Confrontational and coercive techniques can damage relationships, breeding mistrust, anger, resentment, and hostility. Competitive approaches, since they undermine trust and relationships, inhibit the open sharing of information necessary to achieve joint gains. So this approach produces the sort of exchange that prevents the development of collaborative solutions that satisfy both parties.[41]

COLLABORATIVE APPROACHES

Collaborative approaches, by contrast, attempt to find integrative solutions that produce maximum joint gains. In some cases, integrative solutions are easy to produce, such as when parties want opposite things that don't cancel each other out. A classic fable illustrates this. Two sisters were arguing over a single orange. Finally, they agreed to split the orange in half. This compromise left them each dissatisfied with the solution, since they each wanted an entire orange— one for the juice and one for the peel to use in a cake. If they had simply shared their interests instead of arguing their positions or wanting the entire orange, they could have produced an integrative solution that maximized their joint rewards.[42]

Collaborative approaches to negotiation assume that sharing information about interests will allow parties to expand the "pie" by finding things that can be exchanged to create a solution package. In labor negotiations, conflicts over wages are often settled with a solution package that includes more than just pay. Collaborative communication strategies often involve an effort to find things—other than the central content of the conflict—that can be exchanged to create a solution package. People may

- **logroll,** so that all parties disclose multiple important interests and make trades so that each gets the one that is most important to them;

135

- **cost cut,** which seeks to minimize the cost to the other party of going along with a solution; and
- **bridge,** where parties try to invent new options to meet the other party's needs.[43]

Communication patterns of collaborative approaches reveal optimism that a solution exists, a willingness to work at generating many solutions, a concern for the relationship, and a concern that the outcome meets some sort of standard for a good solution. Here are some examples of phrases that might be used in collaborative communication.

Phrases that communicate a *concern for the relationship:*

- This relationship is important to me.
- We've gotten through other difficult moments and we'll get through this.
- I know we can find a solution that works for both of us.
- We're going to work this out.

Phrases that communicate *a willingness to explore interests:*

- What would you like to see happen?
- What concerns you most?
- If things turned out this way, how would you feel about that?

Phrases that note *areas of common interest:*

- We both want....
- We both agree that....
- We have the same ultimate goal.
- We want the same thing; we just want to go about getting it differently.

People frequently produce a suboptimal solution when they negotiate, though. Fisher, Ury, and Patton, authors of *Getting to Yes,* suggest that one main reason for this is the tendency for people to make premature judgments. Judging ideas during the production phase simply inhibits idea generation. If people feel they are being judged, they can be reluctant to put forth suggestions. As with brainstorming, it can be advantageous to separate the process of inventing options from the process of evaluating them.

The process of generating many, varied ideas also can be stunted by the notion that there is just one *best* idea or one true solution. Another way to encourage people to suggest options freely is to purposely offer alternatives you know are impractical or suggest two alternatives at the same time. Either of these techniques demonstrates to the other person a willingness to discuss many options and that suggesting an alternative does not mean commitment to that alternative.[44]

Before beginning the negotiation process, it can be helpful to lay some ground rules. In general, rules should be designed to keep the negotiation on track and prevent parties from engaging in personal attacks or showing disrespect. Rules might include things such as "no personal insults allowed," "only one person talks at a time," or "when one person talks, the other person agrees to listen." In some cases, you may want to take the pressure off the session by agreeing *not* to come to a final agreement at that particular meeting.

"DIRTY TRICKS"

During a negotiation, people may refuse to cooperate or may resort to what Fisher, Ury, and Patton call "dirty tricks."[45] Common dirty tricks include lying about facts. An entrepreneur named Sarah was looking for a retail space to open a small shop. A realty broker representing a mall owner quoted the lease rate to her for an open space in the mall. Sarah went to look at the space and decided she wanted it, but when she went to negotiate the lease with the owner, he quoted her a price higher than what the realty broker had given. Sarah asked about the discrepancy and the owner replied, "Oh I told her that price two years ago when she first started working with me. I can show you the paperwork with the dates on it." Of course, Sarah could understand how the rate could increase over two years. Still, she contacted the broker to let her know what happened. When Sarah relayed what the owner had said, the broker replied that she had confirmed the price with him right before she told Sarah the rates. When Sarah discovered the mall owner's dirty trick, she resumed her search for space.

Dirty tricks can include other forms of deception, such as people presenting themselves as having the authority to make an agreement when they really don't or people misrepresenting their intention to comply with whatever agreement is made. Other tactics include methods of making the negotiation unpleasant so that other people are motivated to end the process early, even if it means making an agreement that isn't in their best interest. This can be accomplished by subtly communicating personal attacks, such as "You don't look like you're feeling well" or "Surely you must realize ..." (implying that you are ignorant if you don't). People may try to make others feel as if they are not important by making them wait, taking phone calls during the negotiation, or allowing for other interruptions. Threats are also a commonly used tactic. Threats can be particularly damaging to relationships and may backfire by complicating the process of coming to an agreement for some who feel that giving in to threats will cause them to lose face.[46]

When the other party in a negotiation refuses to negotiate or uses a competitive approach, you can attempt to pull that person into collaboration by staying focused on interests and not reacting to personal attacks. When attacked, try not to attack back. If your ideas are attacked, try not to defend them. Instead, look beyond the attacks and the positions to identify the *interests* of the other party. Try to reframe an attack on you as an attack on the problem.[47]

EVALUATING SOLUTIONS

Even when both parties decide to cooperate, it is possible that an acceptable agreement may not be reached. How do you protect yourself from accepting an agreement that you really should reject? Typically, people at least want to know their bottom line in a negotiation. The bottom line is the worst acceptable outcome to the negotiation. You want to pay $2,000 in rent per month for your office. You may refuse to pay more than $2,500, so $2,500 is your bottom line.

Focusing on the bottom line protects you from making an unwise agreement. But it can also inhibit the production of creative alternatives. Maybe paying $2,500 would be okay if the utilities or certain maintenance costs were included in that amount. In some cases, being too focused on the bottom line will prevent you from accepting an agreement you really should take. You may not want to pay more than $2,500, but what if space in the area you desire is scarce? You may refuse a rate of $2,600 because it is beyond your bottom line, but you may find no other alternatives available in your desired location.

Fisher, Ury, and Patton recommend knowing your *best alternative to the negotiated agreement,* or BATNA. Your BATNA is different from your bottom line. While your bottom line is the worst acceptable outcome of the negotiation, your BATNA is the best alternative you will have if the negotiation falls through. Instead of focusing on the bottom line, parties using their BATNA ask themselves about the best alternative for them if they fail to reach an agreement. Using a BATNA as a way of deciding whether to accept an agreement protects you from walking away from a less-than-perfect agreement to an even worse alternative.[48]

To prepare for a negotiation, you should work to develop a clear sense of your BATNA. If you know your alternative to the negotiated agreement and it isn't all that bad, then you're less likely to agree to something that really isn't in your best interest. The better your BATNA, the more power you have in the negotiation.[49]

What other techniques can you use to evaluate an agreement? To ensure that the agreement you're accepting will work for you *and* the other party, you should compare it with objective criteria you've agreed upon in advance.[50] For example, managers and clerical workers may have different interests when it comes to scheduling breaks and vacations. A criterion for a good solution for management might be that only a certain number of clerical workers be away from the office at a time. For the clerical workers, a criterion might be that breaks occur at the same time each day. Whatever schedule is produced in negotiation would be compared with the criteria before being accepted.

Setting standards can lead to a wiser and fairer solution. However, agreeing on criteria can in itself require some negotiation. You can begin by agreeing on generalities rather than specifics. For example, you may agree that you want to set a fair price, create a just rule, produce a quality product, write a workable policy, or simply be able to work together. After reaching this initial agreement, the search for specific criteria can begin. Often, objective standards such as market value, scientific findings, or cost/benefit ratios can be used. Remember that if you suggest a requirement, you should be prepared to explain your reasons for wanting it included. The criteria should reflect the interests of both parties.[51]

MEDIATION

What can managers do when the conflict to resolve is not their own, but that of their employees? Managers faced with employee conflict can ignore it, separate the employees, terminate one or both of the employees, send them to counseling, hire a third party to intervene or intervene themselves.[52] The goal of third-party intervention is to assist in transforming the conflict elements in some way. A manager can use a number of approaches to accomplish this general goal. Managers can alter the degree of interdependence between the parties, change perceptions of goals so they are not seen as incompatible, increase a resource to reduce competition due to scarcity, or alter the perceived or actual interference of one party with the other's goal attainment. Or managers can mediate conflicts.

Managers can act as mediators or facilitators of employee conflicts that require intervention if they are able to remain neutral and if they are of a higher status than the conflicting parties. The goals of **mediation** range from facilitating organizational change to facilitating dialogue to breaking destructive cycles to reaching an agreement in principle to reaching a written agreement.[53] Mediation should not be used to establish guilt or innocence, to discipline or punish, or to decide right and wrong. It is not an appropriate approach to deal with violations of a legal or ethical code. Nor is it an appropriate strategy for dealing with personal problems, such as performance issues caused by substance abuse.[55]

Conflict Quote

Christopher Komisarjevsky is chairman and chief executive of Burson-Marsteller, a global public relations firm. His strategy is to let employees work out their own conflicts. "Every organization has an inherent level of conflict within it," he says. "That's actually a form of competition that's healthy. In tough times, though, some people will begin to react politically rather than professionally," and it can have a devastating effect on an organization.

"Most organizations today are made up of teams," says Komisarjevsky. But "numerous times when people are thrown together, they don't like each other or don't agree with each other." When that happens, he says, managers have a few choices: They can fire one person or another. They can fire all of them. Or, they can put them in a room together and say, "Work it out or I expect your resignations." Usually, they work it out.

"I have a great overriding confidence in human beings and in their intelligence and ability to find a solution if there is an overriding goal." You really need to anticipate conflict when very talented individuals work together, but they need to recognize that "at the end of the day, it's the success of the team that matters." [54]

Mediation, while involving a third party, still leaves the production of a solution largely to the conflicting parties. This is a particular advantage of mediation. Solutions produced in this way are more likely to be integrative since both parties are involved in creating them and are more likely to be followed because each party will have a stake in them.[56] However, because both parties must participate in formulating the solution, mediation is only effective when they are willing and able to do so. Mediation isn't a good choice if people seriously mistrust each other, largely because they will not communicate openly. It also doesn't work if the relationship is weak or perceived as unimportant because the people involved won't be motivated to participate in this sometimes arduous process. Mediation also may not be a good choice if people are extremely antagonistic because they must be able to suspend hostilities and refrain from threats for the mediation meeting.[57]

Rather than solving the conflict for the people involved, mediators primarily serve as listeners and guides for the resolution process. Mediators structure and guide sessions, encourage people to see things from a variety of viewpoints, stimulate the discussion, and educate people about the process. They may ask questions to help those involved explore each other's perspectives and reframe comments in a more positive way. In some cases, they will offer suggestions, and in most cases, they will formulate, in written form, the final collaborative agreement.[58]

MANAGERS AS MEDIATORS

To act as a mediator for an employee dispute, managers should begin the process by holding preliminary meetings with each of the parties in private, just to hear each side of the story. The goal of the manager is not to judge or to take sides but to hear and understand the various views. After hearing the parties' sides, the manager then determines what problem must be solved. This allows the manager to focus the mediation on the business problem at hand and on creating a successful working relationship between the parties, rather than allowing the parties to focus the mediation on things they don't like about each other. At the preliminary meeting, managers can also describe the purpose of the mediation, explain the rules of the mediation meeting (e.g., listen respectfully, take turns speaking), and ensure the parties' willingness to participate.[59]

To prepare for a mediation meeting, the manager should attend to the environmental and psychological elements that will affect just how useful the meeting will be. The location should be neutral, private, and free from interruptions and distractions. Seating arrangements and other aspects of the physical surroundings should also be considered, as should the time of day, day of the week, and time allotted for the meeting. Since the people involved may represent other constituents, the manager may also want to consider who else should be present at the meeting.[60]

At a mediation meeting, the manager should work to create a constructive and positive atmosphere and set the expectations for each step of the mediation. The mediating manager should regulate the discussion by determining the sequence for speaking; monitoring the discussion for sincerity, openness, and understanding; and help the parties involved get back on track if they start to deviate from the process. The manager must watch for rule violations in the meetings, such as personal attacks, and point them out as violations. Managers may call for a time-out to relieve tension if the discussion becomes too heated.[61] The manager can also contribute to a positive atmosphere by noting conciliatory gestures that may otherwise go unnoticed. In most cases, but not all, mediation managers should refrain from giving advice, offering solutions, or stating opinions.[62]

As a mediation meeting comes to a close, the solution proposal, if one has been produced, should be examined to see if it is balanced, behaviorally specific, and measurable. The manager's task then is to record the solution and distribute copies to the parties involved. It is also the manager's responsibility to follow up with everyone to ensure that the solution agreed to is actually implemented.[63]

PROFESSIONAL MEDIATION

Professional mediators will be a better choice than a manager mediator when the conflict is very complex or when the manager doubts her ability to handle mediation or to remain impartial. Professional mediators come from a variety of backgrounds and bring with them a variety of styles and goals for mediation. Some mediators may simply be concerned with reaching a settlement, while others may see the mediation as an opportunity to create change and transform relationships. Mediators with legal backgrounds tend to be more focused on content issues and attend less to relationship issues. Mediators with higher status, such as those with a known reputation, may use reflexive, distributive, or representation techniques (asking one side to state the other's position) because the parties are more likely to listen to a higher-status mediator. Techniques such as threatening, rewarding, information gathering, empowering, and agenda setting can also be employed with a higher-status mediator. However, mediators who examine relationship, identity, and process issues typically produce better solutions.[64]

Some professional mediators use strategies that require minimal amounts of information and consider few alternatives in order to save time. Quick solutions may sound tempting, but they are less likely to address the personal issues that emotionally charge the conflict.[65] Mediators who are most effective at achieving a satisfying agreement attempt to improve the relationship between the disputants, rather than just push for settlement or focus on facts. They tend to be

- impartial,
- empathic,
- skilled at communication,
- good at asking questions, and
- knowledgeable about many different problem-solving techniques.

While professional mediations will vary by issue and mediator, some generalities apply. A professional mediation typically begins with the mediator's introductory remarks. This is an opportunity for the mediator to describe his or her role, outline the process, define the time frame, set the ground rules, and summarize the problem as it has been stated in any briefs submitted before the meeting. The parties will then each have an opportunity to explain the problem according to their perspective. The mediator will then ask the parties open-ended questions to take the exploration of the problem further, attempt to find common ground or goals between the parties, and identify which issues will be settled during the meeting. In this "storytelling" phase of the mediation, problems are discussed in terms of fears, concerns, and interests. In this phase, venting sometimes occurs, and mediators are on guard for that, defusing such behavior when it threatens to derail the process. Mediators also ask questions that probe for interests, such as "What will it take for you to agree?" or "How would you like to be treated?"[66]

Sometimes barriers occur in the mediation process and the most reasonable approach is to call a caucus. A **caucus** is a private meeting between a party and the mediator. Any party or the mediator can call for a caucus at any time. A caucus can be used to reduce tension between parties, clarify interests, explain the costs of no settlement, and so on. If a caucus will take some time, a formal break should be called so the other party isn't kept waiting. And when the meeting resumes, the mediator should explain the purpose and results of the caucus to the other party, although no information from the caucus should be shared unless the party involved in the caucus agrees.[68]

Conflict Quote

The advantage of mediation is that a skillful mediator can often find a common ground for resolution that the parties otherwise fail to recognize.

—Robert Fitzpatrick, Esq., Fitzpatrick & Associates[67]

Participants should agree on the criteria for evaluating ideas, and the ideas produced by the discussion should be checked against them. When participants reach a solution, the parties involved should draft a *memorandum of understanding* that summarizes their agreement. The mediator is responsible for writing the final agreement. That final document should mention each of the parties by name and scrupulously avoid any mention of blame. It should also be very specific in its description of who will do what, when, how, and where in order to fulfill the agreement. It should, additionally, explain any penalties for failing to fulfill terms of the agreement. Such documents don't serve any legally binding purpose but do create a common memory of the agreement and expectations of what will happen next for each of the parties.[69]

Not all mediations produce a settlement. Agreements are more likely when conflicts have not escalated to a heated level. At the same time, mediation is ineffective if the conflict is so new that disputants have suffered very few negative consequences from the disagreement. In that case, the motivation of the parties to participate in mediation may be low. People are usually satisfied with the mediation process because it is faster, cheaper, and more enduring than other forms of conflict resolution. The agreements are more satisfying and more likely to be followed because they are tailored to the disputants' needs.[70]

FACILITATION

Facilitation is similar to mediation in that a third party has the role of assisting the conflicting parties in the conflict resolution process. Facilitation is more commonly used when larger groups, experiencing moderate levels of conflict, are involved. It often takes place in a public context, and people who have expertise in the area of concern are invited to participate in the discussion. Not all group situations are right for facilitation, though. It is most useful when the problems the groups face are complex and not better solved with a unilateral decision. The groups involved must be able to tolerate being in the same space with each other, so it is a better choice when the groups are not polarized to the point of being completely hostile.[71]

It is the facilitator's job to create an environment that promotes participation in the discussion, to regulate the discussion, and to provide the tools—including procedures—necessary for the communication process. When it's done well, facilitation can also help build or improve the relationship between groups. Managers, though, can serve as facilitators only if both groups see them as sufficiently neutral.[72]

As with mediation, environmental or contextual concerns for the meeting, such as the day of the week, time of day, amount of time allotted for the process, size of the room, and seating arrangements should be considered. During the meeting, the role of the facilitator is to help the groups determine the goals for the meeting and to lay ground rules for participation. The rules for groups must accomplish the goals of creating a safe environment for communication, limiting the participation of those who would dominate the conversation and encouraging the more passive participants.[73]

During the meeting, a facilitator helps the groups involved use effective communication tools for reaching their objectives. Providing them with a good set of procedures can protect their meeting from the most common complaints about group meetings: people getting off topic, one person dominating, a few people not participating, and people being unclear about the goals of the meeting. As the meeting progresses, a facilitator can periodically summarize the points the groups have made and clarify any misunderstandings. Facilitators can also help groups see their commonalities by pointing out when those groups agree on something. They can protect the communication environment by reframing toxic comments and by making observations that get the groups to recognize how they are talking about things.[74]

Facilitators, though, are only as effective as the meeting management tools and techniques they possess. Managers can easily learn to use many of the more common facilitation techniques, including:

- **Problem census.** This is a technique for identifying a problem where each person at the meeting is asked to present one problem until all problems have been identified, then the people vote on the items they think are most important.
- **Brainstorming.** This is the classic technique for producing ideas, where ideas are generated and not evaluated in the first phase, and then the ideas with the most merit are identified and discussed in the second phase.
- **Nominal group technique.** The nominal group technique requires members to write down ideas individually, then the ideas are discussed and clarified, and each group ranks the ideas in order of importance.
- **The talking circle.** In the talking circle, four chairs are placed in the middle of the group and only those who sit in the chairs are allowed to participate in the discussion. Observers must take the place of a member of the circle to join the discussion. Discussion does not occur between the observers and the circle, but a member of the circle can call for an observer to become part of the circle.
- **Risk technique.** Evaluating a solution can be done with the risk technique, which asks people to give their thoughts on the risks of a solution that has been produced. After the meeting, a list of concerns is sent to everyone. Those lists are then returned to the facilitator with additional concerns added and the original concerns refined. That feedback is distributed and is used as the subject of the next meeting.
- **Parking lot.** In order to keep groups from getting far off the immediate topics, facilitators can record tangential issues that come up during the discussion on a white

MANAGING CONFLICT IN THE WORKPLACE

board or flip chart designated as the "parking lot." Those issues can then be discussed later when they won't detract attention from the immediate topic.

In addition to using these tools effectively, succeeding as a facilitator can take a little practice. Group dynamics have a way of sucking unsuspecting facilitators into traps that impede any progress for the groups. Facilitators can lose control of the process if the group gets off on tangential matters, and—as a result—they may feel pressure to produce a solution and may try to get there too quickly. The groups may also begin talking about something that they have no power over, a third group, which the groups see as victimizing both of them.[75]

Facilitation with large groups is not likely to produce a solution with which everyone completely agrees. But solutions can be accepted with varying levels of agreement among individuals in the groups. At the end of the meeting, whether the issues have been resolved or not, the facilitator must help the groups find closure by summarizing the progress, clarifying agreements, helping the group agree on the next step, and making sure the group gets a summary of the meeting.[76]

OTHER METHODS OF INTERVENTION

ARBITRATION

In **arbitration,** the conflicting parties have a role in sharing information, but the solution is actually produced by the third party and may be binding, whether the conflicting parties like the solution or not. Conflicting parties turn to arbitration because they mutually agree to empower a third party to settle their dispute, or because they are ordered to do so by a judge, or compelled to do so by a contract. Both sides get to argue their case in front of the arbitrator that the parties select, often from a list of qualified arbitrators supplied by the American Arbitration Association.[77]

Conflict Quote

> *The decision to seek arbitration is sometimes made after a conflict has arisen, but much more often the parties have a clause in their contract committing them to arbitration of disputes arising from their business together.*
>
> —John Allison, Professor of Business, University of Texas[78]

Before a meeting, documents may be submitted to the arbitrator for review and sometimes a pre-hearing is held. During the actual hearing, the arbitrator may ask clarifying questions. Decisions are typically made within 30 days of the hearing and no explanation of the decision is required.[79] In a binding arbitration, both parties contractually agree to follow the ruling of the arbitrator. Voluntary arbitration allows for further arbitration or a court battle if one or both parties do not accept the judgment of the arbitrator. In many cases, the arbitrator is an expert in the area of the dispute and may be able to produce solutions that the parties could not come up with on their own.[80]

Arbitration offers the advantage of putting the process of conflict resolution in motion so that parties cannot simply reach an impasse. Cases may wind up in arbitration because parties do not care enough about the relationship to cooperate. Arbitration is useful when issues are clear-cut, but parties are deadlocked. Arbitration addresses only content issues, however, and not relational aspects of a conflict.[81] In for-profit business organizations, this option is probably not best in most cases, and managers should be wary of conflicting parties who ask for binding arbitration. It tends to promote the idea that escalating conflicts, while not learning how to resolve them, is a legitimate strategy for dealing with conflict because, ultimately, they get resolved through arbitration.[82]

ADJUDICATION

The legal system takes over when it is assumed that the parties cannot reach an agreement by themselves. With **adjudication**, decisions are made by a judge or jury after the legal representatives of the parties argue their clients' positions. In some cases, the legal representatives may negotiate a resolution before appearing before the court. The parties, thus, do not participate in producing a solution, but the solution is ultimately binding.[83]

The disadvantages of adjudication are well known and many. First and foremost, it can be expensive. Around $20 billion a year is spent on lawyers' fees in the United States.[84] The parties in conflict are removed from the process of producing solutions, and frequently a solution is produced that neither party finds satisfying. Legal representatives will take a competitive approach to solving the problem and may escalate the conflict and damage the relationship between parties as they attempt to get the best deal they can. Finally, the system is overused and often abused, in part because lawyers, whose fees are based on a percentage of an award, are motivated to bring as many suits as possible.[85]

Adjudication can offer some advantages in certain cases. It sets in motion a process that cannot be ignored by the other party. If a complaint is filed, avoidance becomes a non-option. In the United States, all citizens are constitutionally guaranteed equal protection under the law, so parties of low power can use the law to level the playing field. The process also strives to be fair, assuming advocates of approximately equal skill. Both sides get an opportunity to speak, admit evidence, and have their cases prepared and argued by trained legal experts.[87]

Conflict Quote

For well over a decade the American workplace has been a veritable war zone.

151

Disgruntled employees and their creative lawyers file countless claims against employers. The only consistent winners in this war have been the lawyers.
—Robert Fitzpatrick, Esq., Fitzpatrick & Associates[86]

CONCLUSION

Conflict is inevitable, even in the best of business relationships. And it's increasingly likely as the workforce continues to become more diverse. But that's not necessarily a bad thing. As we've seen, organizational outcomes can be improved with a certain amount of conflict, and at a personal level, professional relationships can be strengthened. The beneficial or detrimental effects of conflict depend on how it's handled.

We've discussed that for working relationships, where patterns of interaction are established, a conflict can be viewed as an episode in an ongoing communication process. To understand any conflict fully and determine the best way to resolve it, we must look at the entire conflict system. We may determine that a conflict can be solved by increasing a resource or by making a minor procedural change. Alternatively, we may decide that the best, most effective way to deal with a conflict is to confront the other party.

Confrontation doesn't guarantee a successful resolution. We've seen that, when mishandled, confrontation may escalate conflict. Working through a conflict to produce a solution that both parties will be happy with and, at the same time, strengthen the relationship between the parties, requires collaborative communication and dialogue. We can achieve this communication goal by adopting a collaborative mindset, listening effectively, and using positive language. Even when we are acting as a third party to employee conflicts or have employed a professional to intervene, the goal should be the same: collaborative communication.

Managing conflict in a constructive fashion means dealing with disagreement or differing viewpoints in ways that respect the individuals involved. The process of working through conflict constructively can strengthen the relationship between parties by allowing them the opportunity to demonstrate this respect, despite adverse circumstances. The most useful long-term by-product of that process will be shared trust.

Working through conflict constructively also allows us to learn about ourselves as we learn about each other by encouraging us to understand our own perspectives, emotions, and goals. No matter where we encounter conflict—at work, at home, or in a social setting—our message is simple: The techniques discussed in this book can help each of us learn to better manage conflict in ways that promote self-knowledge and build stronger, more functional, more productive relationships.

DISCUSSION QUESTIONS

1. Discuss how communication shapes conflicts.

2. How does dialogue compare with the communication typically used in conflicts?

3. During a conflict it is important to control emotions, yet not ignore feelings. Discuss the difference between controlling emotions and ignoring feelings. Why are emotions so important in conflict?

4. Is it ever advisable to use dirty tricks in a negotiation? When and why?

5. When you plan a negotiation meeting, one thing you will need to consider is the seating arrangement. Should you and the other party sit facing each other, side-by-side, or at a ninety-degree angle along the corner of the table? What difference does it make?

6. Why is it best to know your BATNA and your bottom line? What is the difference between these two? Is one more useful than the other?

7. Under what circumstances would you call in a professional third party to help with a conflict? What would indicate to you that this step was necessary?

ENDNOTES

1. William W. Wilmot and Joyce L. Hocker, *Interpersonal Conflict,* 6th ed. (New York: McGraw-Hill, 2001).
2. William C. Taylor, "The Leader of the Future," *Fast Company,* vol. 25, June 1999. Available: http://www.fastcompany.com/online/25/heifetz.html.
3. Cheryl Dahle, "Don't Get Mad—Get over It," *Fast Company,* vol. 22, February 1999. Available: http://www.fastcompany.com/online/22/toolbox.html.
4. Roger Fisher and Scott Brown, *Getting Together: Building Relationships as We Negotiate* (New York: Penguin Books, 1988).
5. Wilmot and Hocker.
6. Fisher and Brown.
7. Stephen W. Littlejohn and Kathy Domenici, *Engaging Communication in Conflict* (Thousand Oaks, CA: Sage, 2001).
8. James J. Floyd, *Listening: A Practical Approach* (Glenview, IL: Scott, Foresman, 1982).
9. Littlejohn and Domenici.
10. Robert P. Vecchio, *Organizational Behavior,* 3rd ed. (Fort Worth: Dryden Press, 1995), 99.
11. Steven A. Beebe, Susan J. Beebe, and Mark V. Redmond, *Interpersonal Communication: Relating to Others* (Boston: Allyn and Bacon, 1999).
12. Elizabeth F. Loftus and John C. Palmer, "Reconstruction of Automobile Destruction: An Example of the Interaction between Language and Memory," *Journal of Verbal Learning and Verbal Behavior,* 13 (1973): 295.
13. Douglas Stone, Bruce Patton, and Sheila Heen, *Difficult Conversations* (New York: Viking, 1999).
14. Stone, Patton, and Heen.
15. Ibid. Douglas Stone, Bruce Patton, and Sheila Heen, *Difficult Conversations* (New York: Viking Press, 1999).
16. Littlejohn and Domenici.
17. Robert Bacal, "Organizational Conflict: The Good, the Bad, and the Ugly." Available: http://www.work911.com/ articles/orgconflict.htm.

18. Roger Fisher, William Ury, and Bruce Patton, *Getting to Yes: Negotiating Agreement without Giving In,* 2nd ed. (New York: Penguin Books, 1991).
19. Fisher, Ury, and Patton.
20. Wilmot and Hocker.
21. Stone, Patton, and Heen.
22. Fisher, Ury, and Patton.
23. Taylor.
24. Stone, Patton, and Heen.
25. Fisher, Ury, and Patton.
26. Wilmot and Hocker.
27. Beth Nissen, "Overworked, Overwrought: 'Desk Rage' at Work," November 15, 2000. Available: http://www.cnn.com.
28. J. C. Gottman, J. Gonso Notarius, and H. Markman, *A Couple's Guide to Communication* (Champaign, IL: Research Press, 1976).
29. Fisher, Ury, and Patton.
30. Fisher and Brown.
31. Stone, Patton, and Heen.
32. Littlejohn and Domenici.
33. Erik J. Van Slyke, *Listening to Conflict: Finding Constructive Solutions to Workplace Disputes* (New York: Amacon, 1999), 85.
34. Fisher and Brown.
35. Wilmot and Hocker.
36. Ibid.
37. Fisher, Ury, and Patton.
38. Danny Ertel, "Turning Negotiation into a Corporate Capability," *Harvard Business Review on Negotiation and Conflict Resolution* (Boston: Harvard Business School Press, 2000), 113.
39. Wilmot and Hocker.
40. Ibid.
41. Ibid.
42. M. P. Follet, *The Collected Papers of M. P. Follet,* edited by H. C. Metcalf and L. Urwick (New York: Harper and Brothers, 1940).
43. Wilmot and Hocker.
44. Fisher, Ury, and Patton.
45. Ibid.
46. Ibid.
47. Ibid.
48. Ibid.
49. Ibid.

50. Ibid.
51. Ibid.
52. Daniel Dana, *Conflict Resolution* (New York: McGraw-Hill, 2001).
53. Myra W. Isenhart and Michael Spangle, *Collaborative Approaches to Resolving Conflict* (Thousand Oaks, CA: Sage, 2000).
54. Christopher Komisarjevsky, telephone interview, New York, NY, February 28, 2003.
55. Dana.
56. Wilmot and Hocker.
57. Isenhart and Spangle.
58. Ibid.
59. Dana.
60. Ibid.
61. Robert R. Blake and Jane S. Mouton, "Overcoming Group Warfare," *Harvard Business Review on Negotiation and Conflict Resolution* (Boston: Harvard Business School Press, 2000).
62. Dana.
63. Ibid.
64. Wilmot and Hocker.
65. James A. Wall, John B. Strak, and Rhetta L. Standifer, "Mediation: A Current Review and Theory Development," *Journal of Conflict Resolution,* 4 (2001): 370–391.
66. Isenhart and Spangle.
67. Robert B. Fitapatrick, "The War in the Workplace Must End, but Arbitration is Not the Answer," *SHRM Legal Report,* Spring 1994. Available: http://www.shrm.org.
68. Isenhart and Spangle.
69. Ibid.
70. Wall, Strak, and Standifer.
71. Isenhart and Spangle.
72. Ibid.
73. Ibid.
74. Ibid.
75. Ibid.
76. Ibid.
77. Ibid.
78. John R. Allison, "Five Ways to Keep Disputes Out of Court," *Harvard Business Review on Negotiation and Conflict Resolution* (Boston: Harvard Business School Press, 2000).
79. Isenhart and Spangle.
80. Ibid.

81. Ibid.
82. Wilmot and Hocker.
83. Ibid.
84. Allison.
85. Wilmot and Hocker.
86. Fitzpatrick.
87. Wilmot and Hocker.

APPENDIX A: Cases

The Fanning Center for Business Communication at the University of Notre Dame's Mendoza College of Business has hundreds of management communication cases available for use in classrooms, workshops, and training sessions. For a complete list, please visit the website:

http://business.nd.edu/Fanning_Center_for_Business_Communication/ Management_Communication_Case_Studies/

DEERFIELD HOSPITAL SUPPLY

Background Note

Diane Jackson is the new operations manager of the Distribution Center for Deerfield Hospital Supply, Inc., a mid-size, non-union healthcare company located in the upper Midwestern United States. The Distribution Center is a $40-million-dollar-a-year operation that employs 50 people, including 15 minorities (African-American, Asian, and Hispanic) and 18 women in the workforce. Four of the minorities are female.

Jackson, a 25-year-old college-educated woman, was transferred from another operations position in the company to fill this position because of some serious performance problems in the Distribution Center that had resisted previous attempts at improvement. The Center had experienced a very high level of defects (nearly 400 per month) as well as a high rate of errors among orders taken from client hospitals. Jackson accepted the assignment knowing that top management would expect her to improve the performance of the Distribution Center in a relatively short period of time.

Jackson's first few weeks on the job were revealing, to say the least. She discovered that the five supervisors whom her predecessor had selected to lead the Center's workforce had little credibility with the employees. They had each been selected on the basis of their job seniority or their friendship with the previous manager.

The workforce was organized into three categories. *Pickers* identify supplies by code numbers in the storage area, remove packaged items from the shelves, and sort them into order baskets. *Drivers* operate forklifts and electric trucks, moving baskets and boxes of supplies to different locations within the distribution center. *Loaders* transfer supplies onto and off of the forklifts and delivery trucks.

Jackson found that her employees were either demoralized or had tough, belligerent attitudes toward management and other employees. Part of the problem, she soon learned, was a lax approach to background checks and prior job references. Five employees were convicted felons, two of whom had been imprisoned for violent assaults on their victims. The previous manager had made all of the hiring decisions by himself without bothering to check on the applicants' references or backgrounds.

Jackson soon discovered that it was not unusual for employees to settle their differences with their fists or to use verbally abusive language to berate people who had offended them. Her predecessor had unintentionally encouraged these disruptive activities by staying in his office and not being available to the other workers. He had relied largely on his discredited supervisors to handle their own disciplinary problems. Before long, the Center employees felt they could handle their own affairs in any way they wanted, without interference from management.

The Loading Dock Incident

While sitting in her office one morning, planning to make several policy changes to improve the efficiency of the Distribution Center, one of Jackson's supervisors entered and reported that two of the loaders had just gotten into a heated dispute, and the situation on the loading dock was very tense. The dispute was between Edwin Williams, a black, male employee, and Buddy Thomas, a white, male employee, and focused on which radio station to play on the loading dock sound system. Williams is the only black employee who works on the loading dock. The company's policy permits employees to listen to music while they work and, in recent years, workers have considered listening to music to be a benefit that improves their working conditions.

Williams insisted that he couldn't stand to listen to the country-western music that Thomas preferred to play. For his part, Thomas claimed that Williams' rap music was offensive to him and made working conditions difficult. An emotional and angry argument developed between the two men over their choices in music, and each yelled racial slurs at the other. Neither the company nor the division had a policy governing the choice of music permitted in the workplace. Apparently, whoever arrived at work first chose the music for the day.

Both Thomas and Williams were known as tough employees who had previous disciplinary problems at Deerfield Hospital Supply. Thomas had been incarcerated for 18 months prior to being hired by the company. Jackson knew that she should take immediate action to resolve this problem and to avoid a potentially volatile escalation of the conflict. Her supervisors told Jackson that, in the past, the previous manager would simply have hollered at the two antagonists in the conflict and then departed with no further action.

Jackson's objectives in resolving the conflict include the establishment of her own control in the workplace. She knew that she would have to change "business as usual" in the Distribution Center so that employees would respect her authority and would refrain from any further unprofessional conduct.

Resolving the Problem

In determining the most appropriate solution to the situation that Diane Jackson faces, you may wish to consider these questions:

1. What are the most important issues Ms. Jackson faces today? Which is most critical?

2. Can you identify the cause of the conflict?

3. What should Ms. Jackson do to settle the conflict? Should either or both of the employees be punished for their behavior?

4. What can Ms. Jackson do over the long term to ensure that incidents such as the one described in this case are less likely to occur?

5. What role (if any) do gender, ethnicity or age play in this situation?

6. What can Ms. Jackson do to develop a group of supervisors who can provide the support she requires and who can properly direct the work of the employees in the Distribution Center?

7. How important is communication in this case? What should Ms. Jackson do to improve the quality of communication in the Distribution Center?

This case was prepared by Ms. Kay Wigton with the assistance of James S. O'Rourke, Concurrent Associate Professor of Management, as the basis for class discussion rather than to illustrate either effective or ineffective handling of an administrative situation. Personal and corporate identities have been disguised. Used here by permission.

SMARTART

SmartArt is a small advertising company that produces socially
responsible advertising (meaning that they do not produce ads for products
deemed harmful to society, nor do they use potentially harmful images in
their ads). Advertising is a very creative and highly competitive field. In an
attempt to gain a competitive edge, SmartArt assigns all clients to client
service teams. To help foster a sense of relationship with the company in the
client, the agency has a policy that each team has one person designated as
the account manager who handles all direct communication with that team's
clients. SmartArt thinks their clients have more confidence and trust in the
organization, because they have consistent communication with one person
they get to know fairly well.

The Characters:

Jane: Jane is the account manager for her team. She has been with SmartArt
for over fifteen years. She has an associate's degree in business and has
worked her way up from a clerical position to account manager. In part, her
success is due to her follow-through; she does what she says she's going to.
Jane is a "by-the-book" sort of person. Her clients like dealing with her
because they know what to expect. Her team, on the other hand, appreciates
the fact they can rely on her, but find her a little rigid. They would like her to
be a little more flexible about things, and they sometimes feel she misses the
forest for the trees.

Paul: Paul is the creative element on Jane's team. He is very talented in both
his artwork and verbal expression. He has been with the organization for one
year. He was a double major in college with a degree in marketing and fine
art. Like many bright, creative people, Paul's work style is a bit spontaneous
and sporadic. When he's inspired, he does great work. When he's not, his
work is a little a flat. His teammates appreciate his creative genius (and they
really do think he has genius), but they wish he was more linear in his work

schedule. Occasionally the team has been pushed uncomfortably close to a deadline, waiting for Paul to deliver on his promise of a great idea.

Pat: Pat is one of the partners at the agency. The agency is structured so that teams are assigned to partners. Jane and Paul's team is assigned to Pat. Pat knows that teams inevitably experience conflict, and she has a healthy respect for how conflict can improve the team's performance and strengthen the relationships between the team members. She also recognizes that when conflicts become destructive, the team, the clients, and the agency suffer.

The Critical Incident:

Jane answered her phone, and on the line was one of her new clients. "I don't know what's going on, but I just spent nearly an hour on the phone with your creative director talking about the redo of the print ads that we already discussed. I thought you were supposed to be handling all of that! I don't have time to tell *you* what I want, and then turn around and have to tell somebody else the same thing all over again."

Jane was furious. Paul had apparently gone around her and contacted the client on his own. And that was the worst thing he could have done with *this* client. The client sold hardware and fasteners to manufacturers. He wanted advertising to place in trade journals and guidebooks for trade shows. He thought simply describing his fasteners was about as exciting and creative as he cared to get, and the edginess of the work in Paul's portfolio made him uncomfortable from the start. He had gone with the agency because he was confident in Jane, and she assured him that Paul could produce something that would meet his needs.

Paul's first pass at the print ads had been way off, and now he can't seem to figure out how to do them over with screwing up the entire deal. Jane could sense that the client's confidence in her and the entire agency was shaken. She was particularly upset that Paul would jeopardize the account after she had worked so hard to sell him to a client that didn't really want him.

After Jane hung up the phone, she took a few deep breaths and headed for Paul's office. He was sitting at his computer and looked up at her as she came in.

> **Jane:** Why in the world did you call ZB Fasteners? You've managed to get Bill so upset, he's ready to move to another agency. I can't believe you would do this to the team.

> **Paul:** Look, I just wanted to talk to the guy -

> **Jane:** It's pretty simple Paul, you aren't supposed to "talk to the guy." You aren't supposed to call the client. I speak to the client, not you.

> **Paul:** You know what Jane, that's fine. Whatever.

> **Jane** (offended by his response): Yes, I know it's fine. It's the policy and it's been the policy since way before you were here.

Jane left Paul's office, calling him an arrogant #@$% under her breath as she stormed down the hall. She was even angrier than she had been when she went to see him, and now Paul was angry as well.

Paul's Reaction:

Paul had nothing more to say to Jane, but he had plenty to say to Pat. He was tired of Jane's controlling style. It was her controlling nature that made it necessary for him to call the client in the first place. While it is true that company policy stated only one person from the team should serve as the primary contact for clients, other teams at the agency had team and client meetings, where all the members of the team got to interact with clients. Jane rarely invited any team members to meetings with clients, and no team members had met anyone from ZB except Jane.

When Jane originally described what the client wanted to Paul, he thought he understood it pretty well. He produced a series of print ads he thought were right on target – but they weren't. The client hadn't liked them and rejected the entire series. Jane had come back to Paul with some feedback from ZB – and a demand for speed. The client had some important trade shows coming up soon and needed to have the ads for the programs done quickly. They didn't have time for another "do-over," so Paul called the client. He needed to be clear about what they wanted and to get Bill's reaction to his initial ideas before he wasted time on something that wouldn't work. He also thought he might be able to talk Bill into accepting ads that had a little more excitement and edge.

Paul felt that if Jane hadn't been so controlling and had let the team meet with the client in the first place, he would have understood the client's needs from the start and would not have had to make the call.

Paul was talented and knew it. He had chosen SmartArt because he respected their mission, but he knew he had standing offers at other agencies. He had already been thinking that Jane's work-style was tough for him to deal with. She never gave him any recognition or showed appreciation for his work. She was very narrow in her thinking and was always focused on schedules and budgets.

He needed to talk to Pat. He would insist upon moving to a different team, and if that wasn't possible he would very likely quit.

Pat's get involved:

Pat was working and enjoying the day, when her contentment was interrupted by Paul bursting into her office. He was visibly upset. He began to complain about Jane being a narrow-minded control freak and said he couldn't work with her anymore.

Pat just listened. She tried not to form too much of an opinion of the problem before hearing Jane's side of things. After Paul left, she called Jane.

Jane was surprised when she answered the phone and Pat was on the line –and livid when Pat explained she wanted to see her regarding some things that Paul had brought to her attention. After Paul violated company policy, he had the audacity to go complain to Pat. It was a lucky thing for Paul that he wasn't in the hall as she walked to Pat's office.

When Jane arrived at Pat's office, she was hardly able to contain her anger.

Pat: So Jane, what's going on with you and Paul?

Jane: Well, right now it's damage control. I'm trying to control the damage that he's trying to do.

Pat: What happened?

Jane proceeded to tell Pat her side of the story. After Jane left, Pat had several concerns. She didn't want to lose Paul, a talented, creative person, but moving him to another team would be very complicated. Since clients were handled by teams, moving Paul meant a whole group of clients would lose their creative lead, and a whole different set of clients would have a new one. At the same time, she wanted Jane's team to work well together. Finally, she definitely didn't want to lose a new client.

Discussion Questions

1. How does brining in a third party (Pat) affect this conflict? When is it advisable to bring in a third party and when is it not?

2. What are the interests of the different parties? Are their interests different from their positions? Do they have any interests in common?

3. Who are the stakeholders in the conflict that my not directly participate in the conflict communication and what are their interests?

4. What sources of power do the parties in the conflict have? Is one party more powerful than the other?

5. What is known about the personalities and work styles of Jane and Paul that could contribute to this conflict? How can personality differences of this sort be bridged so that people can work together effectively?

6. Consider the dialogue between the parties. How is the language the parties use contributing to the conflict?

7. What are the situational or contextual factors that are contributing to the conflict in this case?

8. What options are open to Pat and what will be the aftermath of each option? What should she do?

BREAKING UP IS HARD TO DO

In the small back office of the WingSpot, Ryan Burns, co-owner of the restaurant, printed out two spreadsheets he intended to use to make an argument for expansion to his business partner Chase Freely. It was Sunday morning and Ryan had asked Chase to meet him at the restaurant an hour before any of the staff would arrive so they could talk. He was a bit surprised that Chase had agreed to the meeting without asking any questions.
Ryan poured himself a cup of freshly brewed coffee and sat at the bar to wait for Chase. He looked around and marveled at his surroundings. He had never expected to be an entrepreneur. When they met, Ryan and Chase were both EMBAs.

They met in the fall of their first year of studies at a hangout near campus during a dart tournament and they became fast friends. They got along very well, despite their different backgrounds. Ryan was from a working class family and Chase had a very privileged background – private schools, nice clothes, expensive car. Ryan was studious and made good grades. Not so for Chase.

What Chase lacked in academics, he made up for in social skills. He was confident and outgoing, and despite the regular spoiling by his parents, he had an extremely likable personality. His good looks didn't hurt his popularity either.

Chase had been the one with the idea for the business. It had actually grown out of a project he completed for a class. The business idea was a very simple: a restaurant focusing on chicken wings, hot sandwiches, and wide selection of beers. The concept was nothing unique, but Chase had a great idea for the location. About thirty minutes from campus sat a highly industrial community with a number of factories running three shifts. There were a few fast food restaurants in the area and a couple of old, neighborhood bars; but no sports bars with big screens, bright lights, and music, and no restaurants selling the ever-popular hot wing.

Chase thought a wings bar would do well in the area. The place would attract folks as they got off work from the nearby industrial parks and were looking for a place to relax and get a cheap meal. It would also pull people in on the weekends who wanted to get out of the house and watch a game.

During their last several months of school, Ryan and Chase did their research and preparation. They quit their full time jobs and opened the restaurant two weeks after their last final exam.

They reduced startup costs by renting an existing building and leasing their kitchen equipment. They were able to find used tables and chairs for the dining area on E-bay from a restaurant that was closing down. They rented a U-Haul truck, drove one hundred miles to pick up the furniture, and saved thousands of dollars compared to buying new.

Even so, start-up costs were considerable – deposits on leases and utilities, costs for remodeling the space, office equipment, their liquor license, and signage added up fast. Chase put up most of the start-up money, although it really came from his parents. Ryan didn't have any savings, but Chase knew that when they started. In order to contribute something, Ryan sold the few things he had of value, including a Gipson Les Paul guitar that he rarely played anymore. It had been given to him by his father, so parting with it was tough, but worth it, he thought. He also sold his car and bought an old, but reliable, Honda Civic.

These sacrifices yielded a total of about $7000.00 that Ryan could contribute toward the startup costs. That didn't compare to Chase's investment of nearly $30,000, and Ryan felt bad about that. He argued that they should try to get a small business loan so they could both be equally invested, but Chase wasn't interest in going through the paperwork required to apply for a loan. Chase had complained, "I don't want to do anything that formal and I don't want to be tied so some business loan." Ryan supposed there was some sense in that.

It turned out, at least in Ryan's mind that the investment had evened out over time, because he was the one who did nearly all the work, including all the kitchen management and office responsibilities. He put in long hours, arriving well before the restaurant opened and staying long after it closed.

That's not to say that Chase didn't play a role. He was the face and personality of the place. On any given evening you could find Chase shooting the breeze with customers at the bar or teaching some kids to play darts while their parents finished their meal. He also helped the bartender when the bar was packed and occasionally carried out some food to a table, but that was about the extent of his work.

The bar did well from the start. Ryan and Chase had drawn equal salaries from the bar revenues and still had a profit. However, they hadn't paid back any of Chase's initial investment yet, because they had put money into a few upgrades, hired more wait and kitchen staff, and saved about $20,000 for future investment.

Then the economy spiraled and the community changed. Several of the factories that employed WingSpot customers closed and the bar didn't get the after shift rush like it used to. It was still doing okay, but not nearly as well as it had been, and Ryan and Chase had even had to cut back their salaries.

This couldn't have come at a worse time for Ryan, because he had recently learned that he and his wife of one year were expecting their first child. They had purchased their first home in order to take advantage of the buyer's market only months before, and now had a lot to do to get ready for the baby.

Ryan thought the best idea for making more money was to open another restaurant in a nearby community. He had found a very promising location; one that could potentially produce higher sales than their current store. Ryan felt like he could split his time between the two locations, and he and Chase would essentially double their salaries.

Ryan saw Chase's car pull into the parking lot. He felt a little knot develop in his stomach. Ryan had been bringing the idea of expansion up to Chase for weeks, but every time he did he got a weird vibe from Chase, who always changed the subject.

Ryan couldn't see any reason why Chase would object to the idea of a second restaurant, since they had a proven track record and another store could conceivably double their income. Chase's only objection might be fronting the costs to open another store – and that was required. Ryan had already gone to two different banks and talked to some folks at SCORE about getting a small business loan, but with the economic crisis in full swing, credit was tight, and bars and restaurants were on the bottom of the lending totem pole. So he knew he would have to convince Chase or expansion was out of the question.

"Hey, Ry." Chase greeted Ryan as he came in and set his Venti cup from Starbucks on the bar.

They spent a few minutes engaged in small talk about how their favorite teams had played the previous day, then Ryan got serious and said, "I want to talk about expanding and really hammer out a plan."

Chase's face visibly tensed. The little knot in Ryan's stomach grew to a medium size. Immediately, before Chase could speak, Ryan said, "Look, we know that eventually the economy is going to turn around, so things are only going to get better, not worse."

Chase sighed wearily. That was uncharacteristic of the always energetic, outgoing charmer. "Well, I don't think we can say that we know that. No one can *know* that."

"It's a reasonable assumption." Ryan argued. "And we're doing pretty well as it is, all things considered. We've seen that even when times are bad, people still want to watch sports and drink beer."

"Look, Ry," Chase straightened his spine, "This just isn't working for me anymore."

Ryan's face crinkled in confusion. "What do you mean? What's not working?"

"I mean this whole thing; the restaurant, this podunk town. I've had enough of it. I'm ready to move on."

"I don't get that – 'you've had enough of it.' This is a business, not a bowl of guacamole; how can have you have had enough of it? We've only been doing this for four years! And we've been successful."

"Look, I never intended to do this forever – and you never intended to do it all. I had the idea remember. So, don't talk about this like this was ever a dream career for either one of us."

"What the hell, Chase? Who thinks about dream careers? My dream career is to play guitar for the next Rolling Stones, but that ain't gonna happen. What would you do instead of this?"

"I'm going to work for my dad's company."

Ryan's medium sized stomach knot doubled in size. Chase had always had this option and it was an attractive one. He'd make good money, he'd travel to exciting cities, and he'd be the boss of his team. In the past, he'd avoided committing to working for his dad, because he wasn't ready for the responsibility it would bring. He had preferred to hang out in the bar environment. But now maybe he was tiring of that.

"So what are you saying? What about the bar?"

"I want out. I've been talking to a guy who's interested in buying the place."

Ryan was dumfounded, "You've talked to someone? You talked to someone else, before you talked to me?"

Chase looked a little guilty. "He brought it up, not me – some guy that's been in here a few times. He just asked about it out of the blue. Look, you can get a loan and buy me out, if you want to keep doing this."

Ryan already knew he couldn't get a loan. "What if I buy you out over time with interest?" he proposed.

"I can't do that."

Ryan's mood took a sudden turn toward anger. "Why not? You're going to be making plenty of money working for your dad."

"Ryan, you need to open your eyes. This place is going down. Sales are going down. The economy is down. It's getting worse and it isn't going to get any better soon."

"What are you saying you don't trust me? You don't think I would pay you?" Ryan looked disgusted. "I thought you had more respect for me than that. Hell, I thought we were friends."

"We are friends. It's not about that. It's not about trusting you. You can't change the economy. We've got customers coming in here, paying for chicken wings with their unemployment money. That's going to run out at some point. I don't have any faith in the place surviving, especially if I'm not here. Let's sell it while we can."

"What if I refuse to sell?"

"If you don't want to sell the place, then you need to buy me out."

"How much will it take for me to buy you out?"

"The only thing I want is my initial $30,000 back."

"What about all the hours that I've spent working, while you were out here drinking? I've carried the entire workload of this place ever since day one. I think that should count against some of that capital investment."

Chase looked incredulous. "Do you think that all those hours I've spent here entertaining customers that there wasn't anywhere else I'd rather have been or anything else I'd rather have been doing? Or all that time I spent on the road, finding vendors and building relationships with our suppliers. That was work, too."

Ryan sneered. It wasn't the same thing and Chase knew it, but he would never admit it. In the end he was spoiled and stubborn, just like he had been raised to be.

"What if I can't get a loan for $30,000?" Ryan asked.

"It doesn't have to be for that much. I can take the $20,000 we've got saved and then you owe me less than $10,000. You could get a loan for that."

No, I can't, Ryan thought. He was running numbers in his head. Without paying Chase, would he be able to make enough with one restaurant? Could he get by without the $20,000? Could he really run the place without help after the baby came? Maybe not. And if he hired an assistant manager, then he would be back to not taking home enough income.

His head was spinning and it started to ache. "I can't believe you are doing this to me," he said, more loudly than he had intended.

Chase raised his voice in response. "I'm not doing anything to you. This is business, it isn't personal. Nobody ever said anything about this being a lifetime commitment."

"Dammit, Chase, how can you say it's not personal? You are @#$%ing up my entire life, and you're telling me that it's not personal?" Ryan was up and pacing around now.

"Ryan, you need to calm down."

"Don't tell me to calm down!"

"Seriously, buddy –"

"Seriously? The problem with you Chase is that you don't know anything about being serious. This has just been a fun little hobby for you, and now you're tired of it, so you just run back to mommy and daddy. But what am I supposed to do? I can't get another job around here right now."

"I can't help that."

"But you can help making a decision like this without even talking to me about it. How long have you known you were going to this?"

Before Chase had time to respond, Carla, the head cook opened the back door. She stopped in the hallway and looked down the hall at the two men. She could tell something was off. Ryan stormed down the hall and pushed past Carla.

As he headed out the door, he yelled over his shoulder, "I'm getting a lawyer."

"That's an incredibly stupid thing to do, Ryan," Chase replied loudly.

Carla and Chase heard Ryan's tires squeal as he pulled out of the parking lot.

Discussion Questions

1. What are the interests of Ryan and Chase? Do they have any common interests?

2. Should Ryan and Chase invite a third party into this conflict? If so, what role should that person play? If they were to seek mediation, how would they go about finding a mediator?

3. If Ryan decides to negotiate with Chase rather than meeting with a lawyer, how should he prepare for that conversation?

4. What situational and contextual factors are contributing to this conflict?

5. What are Ryan's options? How do you think he should proceed?

BULLSEYE

Jessica picked up the phone and dialed the first three numbers of the four digit extension to the Director of Human Resources, and then hung the phone up before dialing the last number. "I ought to be able to handle this on my own," she thought, but she had no idea where to begin. Jessica was still reeling from the shocking news one of her newest employees had delivered moments before.

Amber Finch had just informed Jessica that a group of her direct reports and their families had held a barbeque over the weekend at the home of Kevin Beck, an employee in Jessica's department with just over nine years on the job. The featured event for the adults at the party was a dart tournament in set up in Kevin's garage. Given a different context, Jessica might have thought it sounded like a fun time. But the devil was in the details of this story. The organizers of the party had purchased a number cork boards to make their own large dart boards for the tournament. Then they had proceeded to print headshots of Jessica and five members of her team from the company website. They had attached the headshots to the cork with the noses marked as the bull's-eye. Then, tournament players took turns throwing darts at the faces of their coworkers.

Jessica Newman was a thirty-two year old go-getter who had worked for two companies since earning her joint MBA and MSIT at twenty-six. She had been with her current company, Wyba, Inc., a global manufacturer of medical products and equipment, for five years and been in her current position, as IT Manager Midwest Division, for three of them.

The problems in the department started about six months ago when changes were made to streamline the staffing at Wyba. Up to that point, the Midwest Division had always had two IT Managers: most recently, Jessica and a man named Gary Brewer, who started as IT Manager about a year before Jessica. Jessica and Gary each had a team of five direct reports. The two managers worked well together, informally dividing responsibilities between their teams according to strengths and interests. The two teams generally didn't work *together* on projects, still no one in the IT department was happy to hear that changes would be made to their group. Gary's team was angry and resentful when it was revealed that the talked of changes involved removing Gary and combining the two teams under the leadership of Jessica.

Upper management felt that both Gary and Jessica were fine managers, but IT is a specialized area. It wasn't as if their particular skills would transfer well to management of a sales group or even a production or quality department, so someone had to go. The decision to terminate Gary and retain Jessica was made impersonally by evaluating a set of materials, including scores on performance evaluations and technology certifications obtained over the last several years.

However, management had underestimated the negative reaction of Gary's team. The team was very resistant to working *for* Jessica and *with* her group. They blamed Jessica for Gary being fired and rumors circulated that she was having an intimate relationship with a member of upper management which had influenced the decision of who should be terminated.

Jessica was easily able to sense the tension in the group immediately upon taking over leadership. However, the group was not openly defiant of her authority. Gary's former team did their work – with as poor an attitude as they could muster – but they did it. The disrespect they showed Jessica was blatant, but not task related. Jessica would often give a briefing in the morning, updating everyone on the current state of various projects. IT didn't have its own conference room, so Jessica would stand in the middle of the large room where the IT employees' desks were all located and give her update. At first Gary's group would continue working while she spoke, clicking away at their keyboards. She put a stop to that, but now the group refused to make eye contact. They would look down at their desk or stare into space. Still, they got what they needed out of her briefings because their work was always done right and on time.

The folks that were members of Jessica's former team loved working for her. In the year before Gary was let go, Jessica's team really gelled. They had spent a lot of time together outside the office and had become a very tight bunch. They rallied behind Jessica and were offended by the treatment she was receiving from Gary's team. They would talk amongst themselves about the latest offense committed by a member of the "A team" – a name given to Gary's group by Jessica's team, who all understood that the "A" stood for a-hole.

The divide between the groups continued to grow as the groups engaged in behavior that Jessica considered extremely childish. They would avoid each other at the coffeemaker, in the lunchroom, and the parking lot. One group would order pizza delivery on Friday, making the entire office to smell like pizza, but wouldn't share the food with the other team. A plant on one employee's desk started to smell like sour milk and it was assumed someone from the other team had poured milk in the planter.

Fortunately, Jessica was able to keep the teams on separate tasks. Since they had previously been on two separate teams, the office space was already set up with the desks of each group on opposite sides of the large room. This seemed to help with the day-to-day flow of work.

Amber Finch was the only new hire since Gary's dismissal, and she didn't have any loyalty to either team; however, she felt some loyalty to Jessica, since Jessica had hired her. Amber, for the most part, tried to get along with both groups and had managed, in her two months with the company, to form a few tenuous relationships with employees from both sides, which is how she found out about the dart party. She wasn't there of course, but she had heard other employees talk about it and after some deliberation, felt she had to tell Jessica. Amber knew that Kevin, called Beck by his coworkers, had been involved in planning the party, but he was not the only one. She didn't know who else had been involved in the planning, but she had heard that all of Gary's team had been there with their families and some other friends.

Jessica was not an overly emotional person, and though she felt disrespected by Gary's team and was becoming increasingly angry with them, she refused to allow her professionalism to be affected by their behavior. She felt that doing something like standing in the middle of the room during a briefing and insisting that people look at her would make her look foolish and ineffectual.

She had thought that if she ignored the childish displays of disrespect and didn't dignify the rumors about her with a response, then time would take care of the problem. Gary's group would get tired of acting up and would start treating her with the respect she'd earned. But now something was happening. Everyone in the office was siding against each other and the energy in the office was about the conflict between the two sides, not the work. Work was taking a bit longer to complete than Jessica felt it should, because people were distracted by gossiping about each other and plotting against the other side. And now the dart party had pushed the level of disrespect to an unacceptable point. She would love to line up Gary's team and fire them all, but that would never work. She had to do something to unite this group and help them move forward from this conflict. It had been hard for her to figure out how to do that before, but after the dart story gets out to members of her original team - which of course, it will - it may be impossible.

You are a friend to Jessica and she considers you to be an important mentor. After deciding not to go immediately to HR, she's come to you seeking advice. What can she do with this group? Can she turn them into a high-performing team? What will happen when her team finds out about the party? Can she help both sides put this conflict behind them?

Discussion Questions

1. What should Jessica's goal for the team in this case be?

2. What attribution errors are being made in this case? Would it be better for Jessica to openly correct them or say nothing about them?

3. What are Jessica's options? What would an effective communication strategy involve?

4. What can be done to repair relationships that have been seriously damaged in a conflict?

INDEX:

ABOUT THE AUTHOR

Dr. Sandra Collins is an Associate Teaching Professor of Management in the Fanning Center for Business Communication at the Mendoza College of Business at the University of Notre Dame. She has published texts in interpersonal communication, persuasion, and conflict management. She earned her PhD from the University of Notre Dame in social psychology. Her research interests focus on the conflict, team processes, and how language affects perceptions. She earned a Certificate in Leadership Coaching from the Institute for Transformational Leadership at Georgetown University and works with leaders to develop their leadership style and presence.

59713701R00108

Made in the USA
Lexington, KY
12 January 2017